WATCH-OUT!

By Ronald L. Waldron

THE CLOCK KEEPS TICKING

authorHOUSE®

AuthorHouse™
1663 Liberty Drive, Suite 200
Bloomington, IN 47403
www.authorhouse.com
Phone: 1-800-839-8640

First published by AuthorHouse 5/20/2009

ISBN: 978-1-4389-7079-0 (sc)

Printed in the United States of America
Bloomington, Indiana

This book is printed on acid-free paper.

Introduction:

I am a card-carrying member of Jewish Voice for Peace because I believe Jews have a special role to play in bringing about a change in American and Israeli policy. The Israeli government claims to act in the name of the Jewish people. It is up to us to make sure the world knows that growing numbers of Jews, as well as our friends and allies, are opposed to Israeli actions we all know to be wrong. I'm not Jewish, but a member of this organization.

More importantly, as long as legitimate criticism of Israel is blocked by accusations of anti-Semitism, it is the responsibility of Jews committed to universal justice to speak up.

Militarism destroys at a higher rate than the seeds of justice arise. Some think that those who speak out against Israeli militarism are putting the Jewish community in danger. I disagree. The struggle for restorative justice for the Palestinian people is what is needed for both peoples. Neither Palestinians nor Israelis can know security and peace without it.

That is why now is not the time to moderate our demands, but to strengthen our demands for justice, to challenge the slowly changing status quo in Washington DC, and to build an outspoken movement dedicated to ending reliance on militarism as the answer to all of Israel's deep-rooted challenges.

1

In April, a large number of people of faith and conscience will raise our voices demanding an end to the use of US money to destroy Palestinian homes, build illegal settlements, and rain phosphorous on the heads of Gazan men, women and children. JVP is part of this effort, and you will hear more in the coming weeks.

Which issue do you keep an eye on?
From day one to day Ten thousand & one, the change agenda is all about reform, repair, and rebuild America. Integrity, ethics, and values Americans can again believe in.

Informed voting: Is it a right, privilege, or duty? What do you think?

Israel Lobby:
Chas Freeman's full statement following his decision not to serve as National Intelligence Council chairman...'The tactics of the Israel Lobby plumb the depths of dishonor and indecency and include character assassination, selective misquotation, the willful distortion of the record, the fabrication of falsehoods, and an utter disregard for the truth. The aim of this Lobby is control of the policy process through the exercise of a veto over the appointment of people who dispute the wisdom of its views, the substitution of political correctness for analysis, and the exclusion of any and all options for decision by Americans and our government other than those that it favors.'

Is the corruption and crimes involved in government?
A.   Republican.
B.   Democrat.
C.   Independent.
D.   Or all the above.

It is completely amazing that for fifty years Washington
has been actively corrupt, with every government agency, congressmen, senator, justice, cabinet member, FBI, CIA, pentagon personnel, media personalities, staffers and any other employee up and down the line

having full knowledge of such activities, that no real attempt has ever been made to change it.

No accountability top to bottom.

Now that the entire government from federal, state and local agency is collapsing down around our ears, all we get at present is lip service.

The same corrupt lobbies are influencing officials the same corrupt financial institutions, with no change in their administrations. They now get larger bonuses. The same no-bid contractors, waste tax payer money.No prosecution for known criminal activity on the hill, nor elsewhere. The same one sided support for occupation and genocide, with despicable human rights violations. The only recognizable change we have seen is Blackwater changed its name to Xe. The syndicate aroma has not changed at all!

No wonder there is no change!
It would take an act of congress, and we never get that any more!

Israelis told to fight 'holy war' in Gaza, Many Israeli troops had the sense of fighting a "religious war" against Gentiles during the 22-day offensive in Gaza, according to a soldier who has highlighted the martial role of military rabbis during the operation. The soldier testified that the "clear" message of literature distributed to troops by the rabbinate was: "We are the Jewish people, we came to this land by a miracle, God brought us back to this land and now we need to fight to expel the Gentiles who are interfering with our conquest of this holy land." The claim comes in the detailed transcript of a post-war discussion by soldiers, publication of which has triggered a military police inquiry into allegations about the use of lethal firepower against unarmed civilians. The use of lethal firepower against unarmed civilians uh, that would be war crimes. Of course it was with the use of American weapons.
Continually provided by the USA. Supported by the religious Evangelicals and Zionist.

The Israeli government claims to act in the name of the Jewish people. It is up to us to make sure the world knows that growing numbers of Jews, as well as our friends and allies, are opposed to Israeli actions we all know to be wrong.

More importantly, as long as legitimate criticism of Israel is blocked by accusations of anti-Semitism, it is the responsibility of Jews committed to universal justice to speak up.

Militarism destroys at a higher rate than the seeds of justice arise. Some think that those who speak out against Israeli militarism are putting the Jewish community in danger. I disagree. The struggle for restorative justice for the Palestinian people is what is needed for both peoples. Neither Palestinians nor Israelis can know security and peace without it.

That is why now is not the time to moderate our demands, but to strengthen our demands for justice, to challenge the slowly changing status quo in Washington DC, and to build an outspoken movement dedicated to ending reliance on militarism as the answer to all of Israel's deep-rooted challenges.

In April, a large number of people of faith and conscience will raise our voices demanding an end to the use of US money to destroy Palestinian homes, build illegal settlements, and rain phosphorous on the heads of Gazan men, women and children. JVP is part of this effort, and you will hear more in the coming weeks.

We must find the inner courage to soften our hearts and seek an authentic peace based on justice and love for both Palestinians and Israelis. Joining Jewish Voice for Peace is a meaningful way to do that.
The Israeli campaign to deny the 1.5 million residents of Gaza their basic right to food has in recent days been showing signs of success.

Israel has enforced a 20-month blockade on the Gaza Strip and has managed to cripple the economy with its recent war that inflicted over $1.6 billion of harm on the Gazans.

Abu Omar Abu Karsh, a chicken salesperson who now sits idly at once the busiest shop in the Remal neighborhood of Gaza City, said that the price of a living chicken had been 10 to 12 shekels (around 2.6 dollars) per kilogram (2.2 pounds) before the war.

The military operations on Gaza, however, pushed chicken prices through the roof "and during the war we sold it for 55 shekels", he said. Israel has bulldozed three of the eleven chicken hatcheries in the strip and severely damaged two of the others. With the lack of production power in the Palestinian ghetto, even relative calm has been unable to influence prices.Chicken meat is now sold at 35 shekels (9 dollars) a kilogram. Chicken is the only meat that the poor can afford but the increase of the prices forced the people to turn away from buying and my sales decreased by 90 percent," Abu Karsh told Xinhua.

While doctors are amongst the highest paid personnel throughout the world, the dire situation in Gaza shows no mercy for even such public servants. Mattar, a physician who works at a hospital in Gaza and has a family of five children, said "I used to buy two slaughtered chicken per week, each weighs 2 kilograms and I used to pay 25 shekels for each kilogram. It is really so expensive." Red meat prices have also surged and the meager humanitarian aid entering the strip does not reach all its residents. The majority of families in Gaza have already abandoned dreams of eating beef or lamb as prices have surpassed 70 shekels (18 dollars) a kilogram.
Living in Gaza is really becoming so difficult, and day-by-day living is becoming so hard. We really don't know where to go and we really don't know how long this will last, and we really get very tired, said Mattar.
The surge in food prices in Gaza comes as hundreds of factories in the strip have already been closed and unemployment in 2008 was pinned at 70 percent.
Since the end of the Israeli war on the Gaza Strip, 90 percent of the population in Gaza depended on food aids they have received from the

Arab and international countries, said Palestinian economist Omer Sha'ban.

Living in Gaza became so difficult and complicated, and I believe that if the situation continues like this, the Palestinian economy in Gaza will completely collapse and poverty will hurt every individual, he added.

Poultry farm owner Ahmed al-Sawaferri said the Israeli blockade has pushed his production to less than half of what it used to be even though his farm has not been harmed by the recent war.

I don't find gas to keep the farm warm in this cold weather, and the limited amounts of gas mostly go to the kitchens and the houses, he explained.

While Tel Aviv has already hinted at its willingness to open another war on the densely-populated territory, Egyptian crackdowns on the entry of sheep into Gaza and Israeli attacks on fishing boats add to the suffering of the Palestinians.

Today, the American-Arab Anti-Discrimination Committee welcomed the Obama Administration decision to seek a seat on the United Nations Human Rights Council. A stark reversal of policy toward the Council in comparison to the previous administration, the move sends an important message to the global community that the United States seeks to be a leader supporting and enforcing international humanitarian law and, specifically, all aspects of the UN Declaration on Human Rights.

The UN Declaration on Human Rights (UNDHR), the cornerstone of International Humanitarian Law, was strongly supported by the United States at its inception. The US should rightfully play a leading role in once again protecting human rights across the globe. The UNDHR, authored by representatives from the United States, Canada, China and Lebanon must be ratified by every member state upon joining the United Nations. Enshrined in the UNDHR are such basic and inalienable rights as the right to life and liberty, the right to be free of torture, and the right to return to one's country among others.

ADC National Executive Director Kareem Shora said "Today, the United States took another brave step toward reestablishing its historical role as a global leader on human rights and rule of law. This is yet another positive step by President Obama and his Administration toward respect for international humanitarian law and global engagement. Since President Obama's inauguration, our government has no doubt taken several steps in this direction and we continue to look for further improvements as we work together to reestablish the rightful image of our nation around the world."

The scurrilous campaign:

The scurrilous campaign against the leading American diplomat on China and the Middle East, leading to the voluntary withdrawal of his name, may have been a blunder of strategic proportions for Israel and her lobby in the United States.

We have been witnessing the awesome exchanges between supporters for Ambassador Chas Freeman and AIPAC legmen for the past few days. Our judgment is that the great American desire to be fair and morally balanced is winning out as usual.

All across the country David Broder's article is saying, "Blair Director of National Intelligence said that the White House told him that if he wanted Freeman, he'd have to fight for him himself. When I asked the White House on Tuesday if Obama supported Freeman, a National Security Council spokesman said he would check, but he never got back to me. Freeman vanished without a squawk from Obama."

We predict that there will be a long and continuing backlash by the American, as well as European, Chinese and Arabian Intelligence Services over this incident. The question is can American Intelligence estimates on Israel and her neighbors ever be trusted again? The Freeman incident is far worse than the incident involving Valerie Plame and her husband Ambassador Joe Wilson in the run up to the Iraq war in 2003. We know now that Israeli intelligence in all probability worked with Italian intelligence to mislead America, the world and Secretary Colin Powell regarding yellow cake uranium from Niger.

The Freeman incident will have a much broader effect than how America went to war on behalf of Israel in Iraq with no exit strategy and little thought to the consequences. How can the Obama intelligence estimates so far as the Middle East is concerned, ever be trusted?

Harvard Professor Stephen Walt, co-author of The Israel Lobby wrote about the Freeman incident this week in Foreign Policy, "It is one thing to pander to various special interest groups while you're running for office -- everyone expects that sort of thing -- but it's another thing to let a group of bullies push you around in the first fifty days of your administration."

Ambassador Freeman himself has cited Shelly's Prometheus Unbound: To suffer woes which Hope thinks infinite?

To forgive wrongs darker than death or night;
To defy Power, this seems omnipotent;
To love and bear; to hope till Hope creates
From its own wreck the thing it contemplates;
Neither to change, nor falter, nor repent;
This, like thy glory, Titan, is to be
Good, great and joyous, beautiful, and free
This is alone Life, Joy, Empire, and Victory.

Israel and her lobby may have won a pyrrhic victory but the real loser is America, Israel and final Middle East peace process that we all so desperately need. This is not the end of this incident. It uncovered the deep fissures in American Middle East policymaking.

U.S., Israel Disagree on Iran Arms Threat:

Senate Panel Told Tehran Has Not Made Decision to Pursue Nuclear Weapons. Iran has not produced the highly enriched uranium necessary for a nuclear weapon and has not decided to do so, U.S. intelligence officials told Congress yesterday, an assessment that contrasts with a stark Israeli warning days earlier that Iran has crossed the "technological threshold" in its pursuit of the bomb.

DPRK blasts U.S. on its human rights. The United States was the No. 1 human rights abuser in the world, the official KCNA news agency of the Democratic People's Republic of Korea (DPRK) said on Wednesday. The KCNA issued an article enumerating the human rights abuses in the U.S., saying it was not qualified to talk about other countries' human rights. The KCNA said the working people in the U.S. were deprived of clothing, food and housing and the election serves only the rich.

US army brass prepare for quick getaway from Iraq. US Military officials in Iraq have said they want a speedy withdrawal of most American troops by President Barack Obama's deadline at the end of August 2010. The second-ranking US military commander in Iraq, Lieutenant General Lloyd Austin, has said he expects to keep about 130,000 American troops in the country through the end of this year, when Iraq has a series of 'elections' planned, but then wants to make a quick exit.

Interpol is examining case for the arrest of 25 Israelis.

Interpol has confirmed that Iran has asked it for help in tracking down 25 senior Israeli officials involved in the recent war on Gaza. Tehran Chief Prosecutor Saeed Mortazavi announced earlier that Iran had asked Interpol to issue international arrest warrants for 25 Israelis charged with committing war crimes during Tel Aviv's Operation Cast Lead in the Gaza Strip.

Six Years of Illegal War: Demand Accountability:

We are fast approaching the end of the sixth year since the invasion and occupation of Iraq, and seven and a half in Afghanistan. There has been no accountability for the criminals who launched these wars of aggression. The current congress and president are continuing both and escalating one.

But awareness and public pressure continue to grow, as does the possibility of criminal prosecution for some of the war crimes. Over 150 groups are asking the attorney general to appoint a special prosecutor for Bush and Cheney. You can add your name or your organization, and find a dozen other easy steps to take here: http://prosecutebushcheney.org

Israeli-Palestinian Conflict

Congressmen from the Unites States recently traveled to the Middle East to evaluate relations with countries in the region. Among their observances was the damage from the recent Israeli assault on Gaza. Participants included Chairman of the Senate Foreign Relations Committee, Sen. John Kerry (D-MA), and House Foreign Relations Committee on the Middle East member, Rep. Keith Ellison (D-MN). Rep. Brian Baird (D-WA) also made the trip. The Congressmen concluded that there is an immediate need for peace and reconciliation in the region and that the United States has a major role to play in facilitating the process.

On Wednesday, March 4th Sen. John Kerry spoke about his visit at the Saban Center of the Brookings Institute in Washington, DC. Sen. Kerry outlined and underscored the need for US leadership in the role of peacekeeping in the Middle East. Sen. Kerry claimed "broader trends represent an opening to make peace possible," indicating he believes peace is possible now, differing from previous failed attempts. The Senator also indicated the peace process while becoming possible will still remain an uphill battle; "The challenge is not what it looks like, but how to get there."

After Sen. Kerry's talk before the Saban Center, a member of the audience asked the Senator whether he would support the withholding of funds from Israel until the Israeli government keeps its pledges of ceasing settlement activity. Sen. Kerry replied that he would not make his policy suggestions public and that his recommendations made to President Obama would be kept confidential. Sen. Kerry's comments imply that he may not be ready to take the first difficult steps on the path to peace.

The New America Foundation hosted a hearing on Representatives Ellison and Baird's trip to the region. During the hearing the congressmen called for the opening of the checkpoints in the West Bank and ending of the blockade on Gaza. Lifting of the blockade would allow for the flow of goods to be monitored, ensuring security which provides a solution to the current unmonitored commerce taking place through tunnels in and out of Gaza. These calls have been made by the international community for some time and are continually ignored. They spoke of the absence of anti-Israel or pro-Hamas sentiments which they had expected and have returned to the United States to spread Gazan's hope for reconciliation and rebuilding.

The Council for the National Interest urges you to show your support for Pro-American foreign policy regarding Israel and the Middle East and to speak out against biased policies in the region, which fuels fundamentalist aggressions against Americans Heartbreaking that the US media never lets the US public know what is really going on--

It has been four years, every Friday, that the western Ramallah town and its community of neighbors have taken to their lands attempting to stop Israeli forces from confiscation for the Wall and settlements.

With the M16s that fire gas bombs at will, along with hand held grenades lobbed by literally smirking soldiers, Bil'in came out yesterday to demonstrate on Friday, a week after they marked four years of resistance to the Wall.

A winding road encircles the town's land on three sides. The gas was fired from all directions before residents even got close to the gate that is the only possible entrance to their lands.

Just 250 meters from the center of town, with another 250 to go, demonstrators were pelted with the gas that mixed with heavy rains and burned the skin. Elderly men were on the ground vomiting, children were ducking for cover behind boulders, but the soldiers were on all sides. The explosions were omnipresent and one had to jump and duck, do a hopscotch skip at times, to avoid being hit with the bombs that fired the burning noxious substance. This week was light on the warfare, with previous weeks witnessing rubber coated steel bullets and live ammunition.

Iyad Burnat, the head of the Popular Committee against the Wall in Bil'in said, "This is a small demonstration this week," yet there were still at least one hundred people at the outset carrying flags of all Palestinian political parties, along with the national flag. They chanted for justice, for an end to occupation. Many demonstrators ran, half doubled-over, to escape the gas that burns the eyes, the skin, the nerves. They also ran to escape the bullets that have come in other weeks.

But it seemed a game with soldiers standing behind the fence that acts as the Wall in this area of the West Bank. Some demonstrators danced and cheered in confrontation to occupation during a torrential downpour. Burnat's wife said, They are stealing our land, they've already stolen most of it. There is no other way to spin it, this is our reality.
It's every day they incur into the town, Burnat says while walking with a crowd of his fellow townspeople. "Every night they come into town, break into the houses, arrest people."

He has been arrested eight times himself. They target all of the leaders of the nonviolent resistance because they want to stop it. Later in a car driving with friends he turns the radio dial, stopping on Um Kulthum. You know why I love only her? That's all we listened to, for two years in prison.

Back in town 26 year old Hamis Abu Rahma is doing remarkably well for having been shot in the head just weeks ago. He wears a stocking cap to protect the slice across his scalp. From just 20 meters away an Israeli soldier shot him in the head and the arm. The third grenade, fired from a machine gun, missed him. He does not remember anything after the first shot as he went into a coma on the ground. For 15 minutes the soldiers would not allow anyone to aid the bleeding man. Ambulances were banned, but friends were able to take him in a car to Ramallah Hospital, a 20 minute drive. Abu Rahma was just meters from his home when shot. Well within the residential part of the village, far enough from the lands of his family that the Israelis have confiscated.

His mother tears up talking about the near loss of her son, a clearly gentle young man, soft spoken while sitting on a makeshift hospital bed in the living room. His hand and arm still shake, but he says he is getting better every day.

All of her sons are back home after stays in prisons and hospitals. The family is no longer able to live off of their land since they are forbidden from reaching it. "We had olive trees, fruit, beans, vegetables."

During this Friday's demonstration Burnat said that 1,500 olive trees were stolen for the Israeli settlement encroaching not only on his land, but the other settlements that surround western Ramallah, growing as ominously as cancer.

Nearby Nal'een Village is active in the nonviolent resistance against the Wall and settlements that are also taking its lands, while Beit Ilo is another town that is surrounded by settlements on the hills around the Rayan home and their neighbors. In the evening the family says they stay in doors. If we walk the streets we risk being shot, Mohammad Rayan says. Travel from Ramallah to his home is severely impaired with their road re-routed by Israeli forces who took the easy route for the settlements.

Western Ramallah is a sight to behold: flowers, greenery, boulders, trees, hills; a pastoral image out of the impressionist period, but marred in the near distance by jeeps, soldiers, guns, settlements: the stuff of occupation.

They break into our house or someone else's in town every night, the mother of Hamis Abu Rahma says while sitting in her living room.

Down the road in Burnat's house his wife says the soldiers come often. Their four year old daughter Manar says she is frightened at night when they break in, particularly when they come to take Daddy. Her plans, for the future? The tiny girl with bright, excited eyes who sports a faux gold

"M" around her neck says, I want to be a doctor to help all of the injured people and the people who get sick from the gas.

Over in the Abu Rahma family home the mother says, "I know this is a different kind of gas they use. They experiment on us. I don't know what the long-term effects are, but I will not be surprised if we develop cancer from this."
After years of struggle she is teary, yet defiant. "No, we will not give up. But what the future holds, I don't know."

Now the Secretary General of the Arab League, Amr Mousa, says that Sharm el-Sheikh is a strong message to Israel that the world is with Palestine. During the major attacks Palestinians from all corners demanded the presence of the UN, of the international community.

Now they have their attention, but to what end?

However the obvious question is who has garnered the most attention. Is it the Palestinian people that some parties note, or is it who will wrest control in an Arab world divided by the internal Palestinian conflict, or is it the western powers who concentrate of the "Israeli-Palestinian conflict" such as Berlusconi who said today that Italy proposes to host a conference on the issue in Sicily.

At the same time reconstruction efforts for Gaza after the bombings and during the ongoing siege are a moot point as Amnesty International and Dr. Mustafa Barghouthi are among dozens who have rightly pointed out that the crossings remain closed and all reconstruction materials are banned.

Oddly enough, out of the initial statements at Sharm el-Sheikh were the clearest words of the day coming from of all people, Egyptian President Hosni Mubarak. Very simple: You should not isolate the attacks on Gaza from the gravity of the entire Palestinian issue which includes the takeover of Jerusalem, the settlements and Wall of the West Bank and the continued control over the Palestinian government in whatever makeup it chooses.

Because the donors are attempting to garner control, the Israelis may play along with them and allow a type of public dual control over reconstruction that retains the Israelis in the position of occupier, meaning with ultimate control and with the local flavor provided by the Palestinian Authority.

And there are the non-governmentally sanctioned efforts such as the 120 vehicle convoy currently crossing North Africa en route from London to Gaza. The aid it is carrying is all on the okay list, it is not for reconstruction. It is purely humanitarian: clothes, food, blankets, some medicines. Yet it remains unclear whether this largest British effort of its kind will be allowed in.

At the same time the official donors in Sharm el-Sheikh, including 71 foreign ministers, the entire Gulf Cooperation Council, the EU and its French president who continues to sing the praises of the western backed President Abbas whose popularity is at an all time low in Palestine. Sarkozy is simultaneously cozying up to the Israelis by putting at the top of his priorities the release of a single soldier captured while engaging in a form of occupying battle against the Strip in June 2006. At the same time the UN Secretary General Ban Ki-moon insists that reconstruction efforts be funneled through the PA and bypass the elected Hamas government, yet still this man who under international law holds the highest office in the land, will not force the Israelis to honor UN resolutions.

This is but a sampling of the circus-like atmosphere in Sharm el-Sheikh as billions of dollars are traded for control of a region that cannot be controlled by anything other than the occupation that has it, and all of Palestine, under its thumb as occupier.

It has been 40 years of occupation of the Strip, two years of siege, months of closure, 23 days of major bombings that have led to the destruction of the Strip whose elected government was never given a chance, was completely shut out by the Americans, Israelis and PA upon the tallying of the ballots.

The unity government that Hamas attempted to participate in with the PA and other parties two years ago was shut out by the Americans and Israelis. It is now said that if current calls are heeded it will try again.

But if the ultimate Israeli intention of its strangulation and bombings of the Strip was to rid it of the Hamas government for the much more publically pliable PA, it succeeded in spades.

But none of this detracts from the circus of Sharm el-Sheikh that has so many fingers in the pot of a 27 mile long Strip, six miles wide in places, among the most densely populated places on the planet, that does not even have control of its own airspace, borders, sea and electricity. No one here is suggesting that the Hamas government and exiled leadership are without blame, but what choices are there when currently political reality is as lost as the history that is being rapidly rewritten.

And then here come the calls: European Commissioner for External Relations calls on Israeli administration to open Gaza crossing…Fawzi Barhoum calls on all participating states to search for ways to deliver aid for reconstruction to Gaza…French President Sarkozy says captured Israeli soldier's release is a priority for France, makes no mention of 11,000 Palestinians in Israeli prisons yet in the same breath says that the Palestinian people are a top priority as far as reconstruction efforts in Gaza are concerned.

President Abbas says we are making every effort possible to ensure success of a national dialogue and the formation of a national unity government while Fawzi Barhoum said the success of national dialogue is crucial for a unity government.

The money flying in Sharm el-Sheikh makes clear one call shouted from the rooftops of the Gaza Strip, Jerusalem and West Bank for seven years: "We do not want money, we want freedom." What the donor conference offers is painfully clear to a population that is in desperate need of aid, reconstruction, but who has struggled for decades for self-determination, for freedom.

The noted Israeli columnist, Uri Avnery, writing about the Israeli case, tried to capture the spirit of Israeli society that produces such war criminals and war crimes. He observed: "This system indoctrinates its pupils with a violent tribal cult, totally ethnocentric, which sees in the whole of world history nothing but an endless story of Jewish victim hood. This is a religion of a Chosen People, indifferent to others, a religion without compassion for anyone who is not Jewish, which glorifies the God-decreed genocide described in the Biblical book of Joshua."

It would take very little substitution to apply this statement to the United States — like "American" for "Jewish" and "American exceptionalism" for "a Chosen People".

Spain's High Court recently announced it would launch a war crimes investigation into an Israeli ex-defense minister and six other top security officials for their role in a 2002 attack that killed a Hamas commander and 14 civilians in Gaza.9 Spain has for some time been the world's leading practitioner of "universal jurisdiction" for human-rights violations, such as their indictment of Chilean dictator Augusto Pinochet a decade ago. The Israeli case involved the dropping of a bomb on the home of the Hamas leader; most of those killed were children. The United States does this very same thing every other day in Afghanistan or Pakistan. Given the refusal of American presidents to invoke even their "national jurisdiction" over American officials-cum-war criminals, we can only hope that someone reminds the Spanish authorities of a few names, names like Bush, Cheney, Rumsfeld, Powell, Rice, Feith, Perle, Yoo, and a few others with a piece missing, a piece that's shaped like a conscience. There isn't even a need to rely on international law alone, for there's an American law against war crimes, passed by a Republican-dominated Congress in 1996.

Likening Israel's occupation of Gaza, to the Holocaust. But what if it's an apt comparison? They don't delve into this question at all.

They also condemn the use of the word "Zionism", saying that "in 9 times out of 10 involving the use of this word in fact smacks of anti-Semitism." Really? Can they give a precise explanation of how one distinguishes between an anti-Semitic use of the word and a non-anti-Semitic use of it? That would be interesting.

Venezuela's "anti-Israeli initiative ... revealingly transcends the intensity of almost every Arabic nation or normal adversary of Israel." Really. Since when are the totally gutless, dictator Arab nations the standard bearer for progressives? The ideal we should emulate. Egypt, Saudi Arabia, and Jordan are almost never seriously and harshly critical of Israeli policies toward the Palestinians. Therefore, Venezuela shouldn't be?

It takes a lot of repetition while an American is growing up to inculcate this message into their young consciousness, and lots more repetition later on. Think of some of the lines from the song about racism from the Broadway classic show, "South Pacific" — "You've got to be taught"...

You've got to be taught
from year to year.
It's got to be drummed
in your dear little ear.
You've got to be taught
before it's too late .Before you are 6 or 7 or 8. To hate all the people your relatives hate. You've got to be carefully taught.

The education of an American true-believer is ongoing, continuous. All forms of media, all the time. Here is Michael Mullen, chairman of the Joint Chiefs of Staff, the highest military officer in the United States, writing in the Washington Post recently:
We in the U.S. military are likewise held to a high standard. Like the early Romans, we are expected to do the right thing, and when we don't, to make it right again. We have learned, after seven years of war, that trust is the coin of the realm that building it takes time, losing it takes mere seconds, and maintaining it may be our most important and most difficult objective. That's why images of prisoner maltreatment at Abu Ghraib still serve as recruiting tools for al-Qaeda. And it's why each civilian casualty for which we are even remotely responsible sets back our efforts to gain the confidence of the Afghan people months, if not years. It doesn't matter how hard we try to avoid hurting the innocent,

and we do try very hard. It doesn't matter how proportional the force we deploy, how precisely we strike. It doesn't even matter if the enemy hides behind civilians. What matters are the death and destruction that result and the expectation that we could have avoided it. In the end, all that matters is that, despite our best efforts, sometimes we take the very lives we are trying to protect. ... Lose the people's trust, and we lose the war. I see this sort of trust being fostered by our troops all over the world. They are building schools, roads, wells, hospitals and power stations. They work every day to build the sort of infrastructure that enables local governments to stand on their own. But mostly, even when they are going after the enemy, they are building friendships. They are building trust. And they are doing it in superb fashion.16

How many young service members have heard such a talk from Mullen or other officers? How many of them have not been impressed, even choked up? How many Americans reading or hearing such stirring words have not had a lifetime of reinforcement reinforced once again? How many could even imagine that Admiral Mullen is spouting a bunch of crap? The great majority of Americans will swallow it. When Mullen declares: "What matters are the death and destruction that result and the expectation that we could have avoided it", he's implying that there was no way to avoid it. But of course it could have been easily avoided by not dropping bombs on the Afghan people.

You tell the true-believers that the truth is virtually the exact opposite of what Mullen has said and they look at you like you just got off the Number 36 bus from Mars. Bill Clinton bombed Yugoslavia for 78 days and nights in a row. His military and political policies destroyed one of the most progressive countries in Europe. And he called it "humanitarian intervention". It's still regarded by almost all Americans, including many, if not most, progressives, as just that.

Now why is that? Are all these people just ignorant? I think a better answer is that they have certain preconceptions; consciously or unconsciously, they have certain basic beliefs about the United States and its foreign policy, most prominent amongst which is the belief that the US means well. And if you don't deal with this basic belief you'll be talking to a stone wall.

Blueprint for Police State:

Seven newly released memos from the Bush Justice
Department reveal a concerted strategy to cloak the president with power to override the Constitution. The memos provide 'legal' rationales for the president to suspend freedom of speech and press; order warrantless searches and seizures, including wiretaps of US citizens; lock up US citizens indefinitely in the United States without criminal charges; send suspected terrorists to other countries where they will likely be tortured; and unilaterally abrogate treaties."

Fuhrer's law:

Legal expert Michael Ratner calls the legal arguments made in the infamous Yoo memos, Fuhrer's law.

Bush Memos Amount to Treason?
The mainstream media have virtually ignored these revelations, though it seems to me this is the biggest news since Pearl Harbor.

Now we can see that these memos laid the legal groundwork for such actions. We knew the military could do this to an individual. We did not know the plan was to eliminate First Amendment constitutional rights for the entire population.
The memos lay the legal groundwork for the president to send the military to wage war against U.S. citizens; take them from their homes to Navy brigs without trial and keep them forever; close down the First Amendment; and invade whatever country he chooses without regard to any treaty or objection by Congress.
These memos lay the groundwork for a massive military takeover of the United States in cahoots with the president. And if that's not a coup d'etat then, nothing is.

If Bush only wanted these powers in order to prosecute a war on terror, why does he need to suspend the First Amendment? Isn't that the smoking gun of a larger intention toward the general population?

So clearly you don't have to act on behalf of another state to commit treason. The Constitution defines it as levying war against the United States or giving aid and comfort to its enemies. It says nothing about the enemy having to be another state.

When the Constitution was drafted, the phrase "United States" barely referred to a singular country; it referred to a new federation of many united states. They imagined militias rising up against various states; it was not necessarily nation against nation.

Surely, when we have evidence Bush prepared the way to allow the military to imprison or shoot civilians in the various states and created law to put his own troops over the authority of the governors and the national guard of the various states, and when the military were sent to terrorize protesters in St. Paul, [Minn.], Bush was levying war in this sense against the united states?

Treason need not involve another state. Aaron Burr was tried for treason. I do think that a plan to control the military, use it in the United States contrary to law and the Constitution and employ it to levy a war or takeover that eliminates the democratic institutions of the country constitutes treason, even if done under the president of the United States.

The authority given by these memos that could be used to raid every congressional office, raid and search every home, detain tens of thousands, would certainly fit a definition of treason.

This would be the president making war against the institutions of the United States.

New Oversight of Pentagon Costs:

A bill to end cost overruns in major weapons systems would create a powerful new Pentagon position director of independent cost assessments to review cost analyses and estimates, separately from the military branch requesting the program. Those reviews, unlike in the current

process, would take place at key points in the acquisition process before a weapons program can proceed, according to legislation sponsored by Sen. Carl Levin (D-Mich.) and Sen. John McCain (R-Ariz.). Last year, the Government Accountability Office reported that cost overruns on the Pentagon's 95 largest weapons acquisitions system
totaled $300 billion even though the government cut quantities and reduced performance expectations.

In the wake of Israel's massive assault on heavily populated civilian areas of the Gaza Strip earlier this year, Amnesty International called for the United States to suspend military aid to Israel on human rights grounds. Amnesty has also called for the United Nations to impose a mandatory arms embargo on both Hamas and the Israeli government.
Unfortunately, it appears that President Barack Obama won't be heeding Amnesty's call. During the fighting in January, Amnesty documented Israeli forces engaging in direct attacks on civilians and civilian objects in Gaza, and attacks which were disproportionate or indiscriminate. The leader of Amnesty International's fact-finding mission to the Gaza Strip and southern Israel .

Israeli forces used white phosphorus and other weapons supplied by the USA to carry out serious violations of international humanitarian law, including war crimes.
Amnesty also reported finding fragments of U.S.-made munitions littering school playgrounds, in hospitals and in people's homes. Malcolm Smart, who serves as Amnesty International's director for the Middle East, observed Israel's military offensive in Gaza was carried out
with weapons, munitions and military equipment supplied by the USA and paid for with U.S. taxpayers' money. The release also noted how before the conflict, which raged for three weeks from late December into January, the United States had been aware of the pattern of repeated misuse of its weapons. Amnesty has similarly condemned Hamas rocket attacks into
civilian-populated areas of southern Israel as war crimes. And while acknowledging that aid to Hamas was substantially smaller, far less sophisticated, and far less lethal ‹ and appeared to have been procured through clandestine sources ‹ Amnesty called on Iran and other countries

to take concrete steps to insure that weapons and weapon components not get into the hands of Palestinian militias. During the fighting in early January, the Nobel Peace Prize-winning organization initially called for a suspension of U.S. military aid until there was no longer a substantial risk of additional human rights violations. The Bush administration summarily rejected this proposal. Amnesty subsequently appealed to the Obama administration. As the major supplier of weapons to Israel, the USA has a particular obligation to stop any supply that contributes to gross violations of the laws of war and of human rights, said Malcolm Smart. The Obama administration should immediately suspend U.S. military aid to Israel. Obama's refusal to accept Amnesty's call for the suspension of military assistance was a blow to human rights activists. The most Obama might do to express his displeasure toward controversial Israeli policies like the expansion of illegal settlements in the occupied territories would be to reject a planned increase in military aid for the next fiscal year and slightly reduce economic aid and/or loan guarantees. However, in a notable departure from previous administrations, Obama made no mention of any military aid to Israel in his outline of the FY 2010 budget, announced last week. This notable absence may indicate that pressure from human rights activists and others concerned about massive U.S. military aid to Israel is now strong enough that the White House feels a need to downplay the assistance rather than emphasize it.

Obama Tilts Right:

Currently, Obama is on record supporting sending up to $30 billion in unconditional military aid to Israel over the next 10 years. Such a total would represent a 25% increase in the already large-scale arms shipments to Israeli forces under the Bush administration. Obama has thus far failed to realize that the problem in the Middle East is that there are too many deadly weapons in the region, not too few. Instead of simply wanting Israel to have an adequate deterrent against potential military threats, Obama insists the United States should guarantee that Israel maintain a qualitative military advantage. Thanks to this overwhelming advantage over its neighbors, Israeli forces were able to launch devastating wars against Israel's Palestinian and Lebanese neighbors in recent years.

If Israel were in a strategically vulnerable situation, Obama's hard-line position might be understandable. But Israel already has vastly superior conventional military capabilities relative to any combination of armed forces in the region, not to mention a nuclear deterrent. However, Obama has failed to even acknowledge Israel's nuclear arsenal of at least 200-300 weapons, which has been documented for decades. When Hearst reporter Helen Thomas asked at his first press conference if he could name any Middle Eastern countries that possess nuclear weapons, he didn't even try to answer the question. Presumably, Obama knows Israel has these weapons and is located in the Middle East. However, acknowledging Israel's arsenal could complicate his planned arms transfers since it would place Israel in violation of the 1976 Symington Amendment which restricts U.S. military support for governments which develop nuclear weapons. Another major obstacle to Amnesty's calls for suspending military assistance is Congress. Republican leaders like Representatives John Boehner (OH) and Eric Cantor (VA) have long rejected calls by human rights groups to link U.S. military aid to adherence to internationally recognized human rights standards. But so have such Democratic leaders, such as House Speaker Nancy Pelosi and Majority Leader Steny Hoyer, who are outspoken supporters of unconditional military aid to Israel. Even progressive Democratic Representative Barney Frank (MA), at a press conference on February 24 pushing his proposal to reduce military spending by 25%, dismissed a question regarding conditioning Israel's military aid package to human rights concerns. Indeed, in an apparent effort to support their militaristic agenda and to discredit reputable human rights groups that documented systematic Israeli attacks against non-military targets, these congressional leaders and an overwhelming bipartisan majority of their colleagues have gone on record praising Israel's longstanding commitment to minimizing civilian loss and efforts to prevent civilian casualties. Although Obama remained silent while Israel was engaged in war crimes against the civilian population of Gaza, Pelosi and other congressional leaders rushed to Israel's defense in the face of international condemnation. Obama's Defense of Israeli Attacks on Civilians Following the 2006 conflict between Israeli armed forces and the Hezbollah militia, in which both sides committed war crimes by engaging in attacks against populated civilian areas, then-Senator Obama defended Israel's actions and criticized Hezbollah, even though Israel was actually responsible for far more civilian deaths. In an apparent attempt to justify Israeli bombing of civilian population centers, Obama claimed Hezbollah had used "innocent people as shields." This charge directly challenged a series of reports from Amnesty International and Human Rights Watch. These reports found that while Hezbollah did have some military equipment close to some civilian areas, the Lebanese Islamist militia had not forced civilians to remain in or around military targets in order to deter Israel from attacking those targets. I sent Obama spokesperson Ben LaBolt a copy of an exhaustive 249-page Human Rights Watch report that didn't find a single case ‹ out of 600 civilian deaths investigated ‹ of Hezbollah using human shields. I asked him if Obama had any empirical evidence that countered these findings. In response, LaBolt provided me with a copy of a short report from a right-wing Israeli think tank with close ties to the Israeli government headed by the former head of the Israeli intelligence service. The report appeared to use exclusively Israeli government sources, in contrast to the Amnesty International and Human Rights Watch reports, which were based upon forensic evidence as well as multiple verified eyewitness accounts by both Lebanese living in the areas under attack as well as experienced monitors (unaffiliated with any government or political organization) on the ground. Despite several follow-up emails asking for more credible sources, LaBolt never got back to me. Not Good for Israel The militaristic stance by Congress and the Obama administration is hardly doing Israel a favor. Indeed, U.S. military assistance to Israel has nothing to do with Israel's legitimate security needs. Rather than commencing during the country's first 20 years of existence, when Israel was most vulnerable strategically, major U.S. military and economic aid didn[1]t even begin until after the 1967 War, when Israel proved itself to be far stronger than any combination of Arab armies and after Israeli occupation forces became the rulers of a large Palestinian population. If all U.S. aid to Israel were immediately halted, Israel wouldn't be under a significantly greater military threat than it is today for many years. Israel has both a major domestic arms industry and an existing military force far more capable and powerful than any conceivable combination of opposing forces. Under Obama, U.S. military aid to Israel will likely continue be higher than it was back in the 1970s, when Egypt's massive and well-equipped armed forces threatened war, Syria's military rapidly expanded with advanced Soviet weaponry, armed factions of the PLO launched terrorist attacks into Israel, Jordan still claimed the West Bank and stationed large numbers of troops along its border and demarcation line with Israel, and Iraq embarked on a vast program of militarization. Why does the Obama administration believe that Israel needs more military aid today than it did back then? Since that time, Israel has maintained a longstanding peace treaty with Egypt and a large demilitarized and internationally monitored buffer zone. Syria's armed forces were weakened by the collapse of their former Soviet patron and its government has been calling for a resumption of peace talks. The PLO is cooperating closely with Israeli security. Jordan signed a peace treaty with Israel with full normalized relations. And two major wars and a decade of strict international sanctions have devastated Iraq's armed forces, which is in any case now under close U.S. supervision. Obama has pledged continued military aid to Israel a full decade into the future not in terms of how that country's strategic situation may evolve, but in terms of a fixed-dollar amount. If his real interest were to provide adequate support for Israeli defense, he wouldn't promise $30 billion in additional military aid. He would simply pledge to maintain adequate military assistance to maintain Israel's security needs, which would presumably decline if the peace process moves forward. However, Israel's actual defense needs don't appear to be the issue. According to late Israeli major general and Knesset member Matti Peled, who once served as the IDF's chief procurement officer, such fixed amounts are arrived at "out of thin air." In addition, every major arms transfer to Israel creates a new demand by Arab states ‹ most of which can pay hard currency through petrodollars ‹ for additional U.S. weapons to challenge Israel. Indeed, Israel announced its acceptance of a proposed Middle Eastern arms freeze in 1991, but the U.S. government, eager to defend the profits of U.S. arms merchants, effectively blocked it. Prior to the breakdown in the peace process in 2001, 78 senators wrote President Bill Clinton insisting that the United States send additional military aid to Israel on the grounds of massive arms procurement by Arab states, neglecting to note that 80% of those arms transfers were of U.S. origin. Were they really concerned about Israeli security, they would have voted to block these arms transfers to the Gulf monarchies and other Arab dictatorships. The resulting arms race has been a bonanza for U.S. arms manufacturers. The right-wing "pro-Israel" political action committees certainly wield substantial clout with their contributions to congressional candidates supportive of large-scale military and economic aid to Israel. But the Aerospace Industry Association and other influential military interests that promote massive arms transfers to the Middle East and elsewhere are even more influential, contributing several times what the pro-Israel PACs contribute. The huge amount of U.S. aid to the Israeli government hasn't been as beneficial to Israel as many would suspect. U.S. military aid to Israel is, in fact, simply a credit line to American arms manufacturers, and actually ends up costing Israel two to three times that amount in operator training, staffing, maintenance, and other related costs. The overall impact is to increase Israeli military dependency on the United States ‹ and amass record profits for U.S. arms merchants. The U.S. Arms Export Control Act requires a cutoff of military aid to recipient countries if they're found to be using American weapons for purposes other than internal security or legitimate self-defense and/or their use could increase the possibility of an outbreak or escalation of conflict." This might explain Obama's refusal to acknowledge Israel's disproportionate use of force and high number of civilian casualties.

Israelis told to fight 'holy war' in Gaza, Many Israeli troops had the sense of fighting a "religious war" against Gentiles during the 22-day offensive in Gaza, according to a soldier who has highlighted the martial role of military rabbis during the operation. The soldier testified that the "clear" message of literature distributed to troops by the rabbinate was: "We are the Jewish people, we came to this land by a miracle, God brought us back to this land and now we need to fight to expel the Gentiles who are interfering with our conquest of this holy land." The claim comes in the detailed transcript of a post-war discussion by soldiers, publication of which has triggered a military police inquiry into allegations about the use of lethal firepower against unarmed civilians. The use of lethal firepower against unarmed civilians uh, that would be war crimes. Of course it was with the use of American weapons continually provided by the USA. Supported by religious, Evangelicals and Zionist.
ARE WE ANGRY YET? REFORM OR REVOLUTION IS EVIDENT. PEACE AND JUSTICE: Dear Recipient(s): Four books

on topic, promote such and raise needed funds for your organization. Contact Josh Fountain regarding such promotion, and wholesale & retail pricing. Book 1. Final Report. # 49149 by Ronald L. Waldron Book 2. Deception. Be not Deceived. # 53223 by RLW Book 3. WHAT IF?? # 60400 by Ronald L. Waldron. Book 4. WATCH-OUT!! # 61438, by Ronald L. Waldron. The American Public Affairs Committee (AIPAC) is the leading player in what is sometimes referred to as "The Israel Lobby" – a coalition that includes major Jewish groups, neoconservative intellectuals and Christian Zionists. With its impressive contacts among Hill staffers, influential grassroots supporters and deep connections to wealthy donors, AIPAC is the lobby's key emissary to Congress. But in many ways, AIPAC has become greater than just another lobby; its work has made unconditional support for Israel an accepted cost of doing business inside the halls of Congress. AIPAC's interest, Israel's interest and America's interest are today perceived by most elected leaders to be one and the same. Christian conservatives increasingly aligned with AIPAC demand unwavering support for Israel from their Republican leaders. There will never be a victor in this conflict but there will always be a victim. It is only a matter of time before the consequences start to ripple in our own country. As long as the United States continues to give Israel the green light for such atrocious attacks, we will be providing justifications in the minds of extremist to harm our nation. It is not only a matter of morals and legal violations; it is a matter of security. The short-term policies of our government toward Israel must be changed. Only a fair and objective approach to the Middle East will bring the fundamental change for peace.

Three Israeli refuseniks, left to right: Ron Gerlitz, a software engineer now living in Cupertino; Ofer Shorr, a translator married to a UC Berkeley graduate student; and Ishai Rosen Zvi, a visiting scholar in Berkeley's Near Eastern Studies department.

Refuseniks: Three Israeli soldiers tell why they will not serve in the occupied territories

BERKELEY - For his required three years of active service in the Israeli Defense Forces (IDF), Ishai Rosen-Zvi was stationed at a checkpoint in Gaza starting in 1990. He didn't see much action there, but the very banality of his everyday interactions with Palestinians began the process that turned him into a "refusenik" — one of the estimated 1,100 IDF soldiers who have signed conscientious-objector pledges declaring they will not serve in Israel's occupied territories.

"We did not meet terrorists. They did not come to our roadblocks," Rosen-Zvi told a UC Berkeley audience. "But we did meet many people. Most of them were very poor. They were just trying to get to their jobs ... I have a vivid picture. It is 4:45 a.m. and the line [to cross a checkpoint] is hundreds, sometimes thousands of people long, some waiting with food in their hands. All their fate depends on some 19-year-old commander. If they are lucky, this guy already spoke with his girlfriend that morning and everything will go smoothly ... You see their eyes. They're looking at you with fear, frustration, hatred. You are their prison guard."

Rosen-Zvi joined two other soldiers to deliver a March 11 lecture at Dwinelle Hall called "Why Do We Refuse to Serve in the Occupied Territories? Israeli Voices Against the Occupation." The event was organized by Tzedek (a Hillel-sponsored Jewish group at UC Berkeley), funded by the Middle East Educational Programs Fund, and cosponsored by the Chancellor's Educational Activities Committee, the Center for Middle East Studies, UC Berkeley Human Rights Center, Tikkun, Boalt Hall International Human Rights Student Board, Students for Justice in Palestine, A Jewish Voice for Peace, and the ASUC. Courage to Refuse and Yesh Gvul ("There is a limit")— the organization of the refuseniks and the network that supports them in their stance — were also cosponsors.

Although the refuseniks' official numbers represent but a fraction of the 1.3 million Israeli males fit for military service — Israeli law does not recognize conscientious objection for men, it does allow it for women — they are making their influence felt in lecture tours like this one. "They say we are just a small minority," said one of the speakers. "We are a minority, yes, but not a small one."

'We shall take no part'

The three men were there to share their stories of what ultimately led them to a position whose unpopularity has trailed them from Israel to much of the United States.

All three have signed the "Combatants Letter of Courage to Refuse," that includes the signature of some 500 soldiers. The letter states that these combat officers and soldiers "who have served the State of Israel for long weeks every year, in spite of the dear cost to our personal lives, have been on reserve duty all over the occupied territories (areas in the West Bank and Gaza formerly under Palestinian control), and were issued commands and directives that had nothing to do with the security of our country, and that had the sole purpose of perpetuating our control over the Palestinian people." It goes on to declare that the signatories will not "continue to fight beyond the 1967 borders in order to dominate, expel, starve and humiliate an entire people. We hereby declare that we shall continue serving in the Israel Defense Forces in any mission that serves Israel's defense. The missions of occupation and oppression do not serve this purpose — and we shall take no part in them." (Read the full text.)

Last year Rosen-Zvi received a routine reserve duty summons for a week-long stint in the Nablus area, one of the occupied territories. He refused to carry out the order and was jailed for two weeks.

'This is not democracy'

Citing his rough grasp of English, Gerlitz read from a prepared statement. He told how he was drafted at age 18, 11 years ago, and spent his three mandatory years as an officer in the Israeli navy. "I believed then that taking part in the defense of Israel was the right thing to do," he said. "And I still do."

The distinction that all three speakers were careful to make, however, is what constitutes "defense." They emphasized their essential patriotism and their belief in the validity of an Israeli state. For his part, Gerlitz focused on the Israeli government's identity as a democracy. "I believe that to refuse to serve is a democratic action," he argued. "Democracy is not just a majority decision. It must protect the rights of the minority, including basic human rights ... Curfews, tortures, checkpoints, closures — these are not democracy. Preventing freedom of movement, freedom to get medical treatment, this is not democracy."

Gerlitz also gave a brief history of the Refusenik movement in Israel. Coined originally to describe a Jewish person who was refused an exit visa from the Soviet Union, the term now applies both to combat soldiers who will not fight in the occupied territories as well as conscientious objectors who refuse to serve at all in the IDF. The latter group includes Jonathan Ben-Artzi, whose uncle is former Israeli prime minister Benjamin Netanyahu and who has been jailed for months.

www.authorhouse.com/bookstore

Betraying His Constituency

The $30 billion in taxpayer funds to support Israeli militarism isn't a huge amount of money compared with what has already been wasted in the Iraq. War, bailouts for big banks, and various Pentagon boon doggles. Still, this money could more profitably go toward needs at home, such as health care, education, housing, and public transportation. It's therefore profoundly disappointing that there has been so little public opposition to Obama's dismissal of Amnesty International's calls to suspend aid to Israel. Some activists I contacted appear to have fallen into a fatalistic view that the "Zionist lobby" is too powerful to challenge and that Obama is nothing but a helpless pawn of powerful Jewish interests. Not only does this simplistic perspective border on anti-Semitism, it becomes a self-fulfilling prophecy. Any right-wing militaristic lobby will appear all-powerful if there isn't a concerted effort from the left to challenge it. Obama's supporters must demand that he live up to his promise to change the mindset in Washington that has contributed to such death and destruction in the Middle East. The new administration must heed calls by Amnesty International and other human rights groups to condition military aid to Israel and all other countries that don't adhere to basic principles of international humanitarian law. Stephen Zunes, a Foreign Policy in Focus senior analyst, is a professor of politics and chair of Middle Eastern Studies at the University of San Francisco.

Every day brings new sophisticated ways of ethnic cleansing of the native Palestinians while expanding the colonial settlements that increasing surrounds the few remaining Bantustans where those of us who remain here try to cling to a semblance of life (and not just the areas occupied since 1967 but also in places like Jaffa, the Negev, and the Galilee). I would like to impose on you to read a few of these case studies that are compiled by the Applied Research Institute of Jerusalem (ARIJ) for the West Bank. You will be disturbed to see extremely well documented examples of the violence of land confiscation and ethnic cleansing. If you review just a few of those hundreds of stories, you will likely ask yourself why there is so little violent resistance! While awaiting International Criminal Courts to finally take-up these cases, we need to think what we can do together. How much can we get beyond our normal functioning and expand our activism and/or make it more effective (while guarding against compassion fatigue). The best answer for most people is to engage in boycotts, divestments, and sanctions based on the Palestinian Civil Society Call to Action and we urge you to join the call.

IT IS OUR RESPONCIBILITY TO INDICT BUSH, CHENEY, AND ALL INVOLVED:

Nearly six years of constant effort, we were able to reach 1,100,000 U.S. citizens who dared to ask their Representatives and the Judiciary Committee of the U.S. House of Representatives to impeach President George W. Bush, Vice President Dick Cheney, Secretary of Defense Donald Rumsfeld and other civil officers of the United States before January 20, 2009. Despite the Bush Administration's commission of the most frequent, flagrant, and contemptuous and deadly assaults on US. and international laws of war, peace and human rights of any presidency in our history, the Congress failed to act and carry out its clear duty to impeach, so carefully woven into the Constitution to prevent usurpation of powers not delegated by the people and compel removal from office and accountability for high crimes and misdemeanors.

Now we have taken the next step to save the Constitution. It's an effort of great magnitude and we need your help.

We do not regret the effort to impeach. We do regret the failure. Inaction by the Congress on impeachment is tantamount to approval of the many crimes committed by the Bush Administration in pursuit of its policies of military domination and the concentration of global wealth in fewer hands.

The failure to impeach clearly exposes the enormous resistance in government and vested wealth to any limitations on their power to commit high crimes with impunity and the extreme difficulty of motivating the public beset by economic insecurity and contrived distractions from addressing its own unhappy condition, plus a sense of powerlessness that is incompatible with the idea of democracy, and incessant propaganda in the mass media confounding the facts. Still there is nothing to prevent our organizing a massive movement of the people that can force the government to act. The Civil Rights Movement forced major reforms that have achieved continuing, if much too slow progress. The peace movement over a bloody decade, 1965-1975, helped force the U.S. government to withdraw U.S. troops from Vietnam, but failed to persevere.

Now we must act effectively to reclaim the Constitution, the Bill of Rights and the rule of law to restore and insure integrity in government designed to protect life and the human rights and dignity of every child, woman and man on earth. This social movement, like all social movements before it, is built on personal sacrifice

Failure to fully investigate, and where the facts found warrant it, to prosecute George W. Bush, Dick Cheney, Donald Rumsfeld and other civil officers of the Bush Administration means they and their successors are above the law and the American people, their government and the victims of their crimes, foreign and domestic, including life, liberty and the pursuit of happiness, will continue to suffer the consequences and assure the repetition of their lawless conduct.

We dare not blink at the magnitude, diversity and pervasive impact of the known crimes committed by the Bush Administration. Wars of aggression in Afghanistan and Iraq, the Supreme International Crime, have killed hundreds of thousands outright, wounded, sickened, and malnourished many more than they have killed and sent millions as refugees to neighboring nations while rendering homeless millions more. Indiscriminate killing of civilians, summary execution, arbitrary seizures of people and property, secret unlimited detention and torture have been authorized widely practiced and both defended and denied publicly. President Bush, the self-proclaimed "decider," reached for unlimited dictatorial power whenever he proclaimed the national security was threatened. And he considered himself above the law where domestic affairs were concerned even as he signed Acts of Congress into law.

A culture of corruption in contracting for security services, war relief programs, reconstruction in war-devastated countries have unjustly enriched favored predators abroad while at home mortgage lenders, banks, insurance companies and corporate executives exploited Bush administration policies intending enrichment of the rich that with the radically increased national war debt and military spending have led to collapse of the global economy, threatening massive unemployment and world wide depression with all their consequences for the general welfare.

Widespread illegal surveillance, at home and abroad, persecution, harassment of and discrimination against Muslims, other minorities and political opposition by U.S. government agencies - the Immigration Service, Border Patrol, IRS, FBI, prosecution by the Department of Justice - have violated the most precious rights of citizens and aliens alike, injured the United States in international relations and cooperation and made new enemies of many nations. Corrupt conduct by Bush politicized appointees, constituting crimes in at least six Executive Departments, most notably Interior and Justice, has brought lawlessness into the government bureaucracy itself, costing billions of dollars and creating distrust of government.

The Bush Administration brought us to the brink of despotic government. A Cheney Administration would have taken us over the brink. The imperative duty of the American people is an unrelenting public demand for comprehensive federal criminal investigations of George W. Bush, Dick Cheney and other officials of their Administration and all persons acting under their authority and direction, followed by rigorous criminal prosecutions wherever the evidence, having been fully and fairly presented to a federal grand jury, results in indictments.

The indictment and prosecution of Bush administration officials is becoming a reality.

A Spanish court has agreed to consider opening a criminal case against six former Bush administration officials, the Associated Press confirmed.

Former Attorney General Alberto Gonzales, former Undersecretary of Defense Douglas, former Vice President Dick Cheney's chief of staff David Addington, Justice Department officials John Yoo and Jay S. Bybee, and Pentagon lawyer William Haynes are under scrutiny for sanctioning torture in violation of the Geneva conventions. Under Spanish law, the courts have jurisdiction to prosecute war criminals and torturers anywhere in the world. A judge has already called on prosecutors to review the charges.

Clearly, millions of people worldwide stand with the mission of IndictBushNow and all those who are fighting for accountability.

PALESTINIANS TO ISRAEL:
YOU
Take my water
Burn my olive trees.
Destroy my House.
Take away my job.
Steal my Land.
Imprison my father.
Kill my mother
Bomb my Country.
Starve us all.
Humiliate us all.

BUT

I am to blame: I shot a Rocket back!!

Indicators of avoidance are what come to mind while absorbing the various rescue, recovery, stimulus and guarantee programs coming out of the Obama Administration to slow and reverse a splintering and shattering economy. If the Obamites do not act now when the political time is ripest, to put into motion forces of deterrence and prevention, the casino capitalists of tomorrow will again be able to de-stabilize our economy.

Alan Greenspan, former chairman of the Federal Reserve, just about predicting another round of recklessness in about fifteen years. But he called it "human nature" not casino capitalism.

Here are seven avoidance indicators which outline what Washington is not doing to prevent another round of greed and misdeeds by the Wall Street few against the innocent many throughout the country.

1. Where are the resources for comprehensive law enforcement against the Wall Street crooks, swindlers and purveyors of costly deceptive practices? Isn't there a need to add two to three hundred million dollars

for more FBI agents, prosecutors and corporate crime attorneys under the Justice Department to obtain the fines and disgorgements which will far exceed in dollars what is spent by the forces of law and order?

Americans want justice. They want jail time not bail time for these crooks. Look how many of the swindled just turned out in a New York City winter to let Bernard Madoff have a piece of their mind as he entered the courtroom and immediate imprisonment.

There has been very little movement so far in Congress or the White House toward this necessary action.

2. Where are the anti-trusters to revive the moribund divisions in the Justice Department and Federal Trade Commision? Failed banks, brokerage firms, and now insurance companies are being taken over by shaky acquirers, often with the encouragement of the federal government. Other industries are experiencing similar mergers and acquisitions in an already over-concentrated economy.

Our government needs to be on top of this accelerating creation of more companies deemed to be "too big to fail." A variety of antitrust policies are needed to prevent, restructure or, at least, require spin-offs to minimize the anti-competitive effects of the "urge to merge."

3. What about Congress and Obama shifting some power to the investors and shareholders who are paying for all these losses? The corporate bosses have made sure for many years that shareholders, who own their companies, have little or no right to control them. Had there been less of a gap between ownership and control, the bosses could never have engaged in such reckless speculation, looting and draining of the trillions of dollars with which they were entrusted. These include mutual funds, pension funds and various trusts. Power to the owners seems to be off the table.

4. The federal officials are talking up stronger regulation and re-regulation proposals but we have not yet been informed of their specific plans. There is not much talk of regulatory prohibition. That is, flat-out prohibition of banks, insurance companies, and other fiduciary institutions from

speculating in derivatives or, to be more specific, bets on debts and the even more hyped creations of bets on bets on debts on debts.

5. By now, Washington should be devising ways to pay for these gigantic deficits and bailouts. A fraction of one percent sales tax on the hundreds of trillions of dollars in derivative transactions annually would produce hundreds of billions of dollars in revenue and tamp down some of this Wall Street gambling with other peoples' money.

Such a tax on speculative trades in these abstract instruments can make the Wall Streeters pay for their own bailouts and reduce some of the taxes on human labor.

6. Our government doesn't highlight not-for-profit institutions like the 8000 credit unions that are increasing their loans and continue to serve over 80 million Americans without a single insolvency. One would think that with the financial goliaths in a free fall, despite ever-larger bailouts from the federal government, that the cooperative model of credit unions would become a useful teaching instrument.

In his new paperback book, Agenda for a New Economy, David Korten makes an important distinction between the "phantom wealth" of Wall Street and the "real wealth" of Main Street.

His twelve-point agenda raises the fundamental question of why Wall Street is needed and how the functions of a just and progressive economy can be fulfilled with a sensible transition to a "real wealth" economy engaged by and accountable to real people striving for the necessities and wants of life through environmentally friendly, more efficient institutions.

Lest any remaining doubters out there are thinking about our country returning to business as usual Wall Street style, please read the confidential PowerPoint presentation "AIG: Is the Risk Systemic?" by the AIG financial giant grasping $180 billion, so far, in federal aid and guarantees

In 21 pages of very large type, you will see why the AIG bosses believe that failure of their gigantic corporation would only "trigger a cascading set of further failures which cannot be stopped except by extraordinary means." In other words, AIG says to Uncle Sam and you the taxpayer save it or be prepared for a global collapse through a dominoes effect of unknown catastrophic sequences. For the full astonishing AIG text, see: http://www.aig.com/Related-Resources_385_136430.html. Right from the horse's mouth!

Huge Bonuses After $170 Billion Bailout :

The American International Group, which has received more than $170 billion in taxpayer bailout money from the Treasury and Federal Reserve, plans to pay about $165 million in bonuses by Sunday to executives in the same business unit that brought the company to the brink of collapse last year.

Word of the bonuses last week stirred such deep consternation inside the Obama administration that Treasury Secretary Timothy F. Geithner told the firm they were unacceptable and demanded they be renegotiated, a senior administration official said. But the bonuses will go forward because lawyers said the firm was contractually obligated to pay them.

The payments to A.I.G.'s financial products unit are in addition to $121 million in previously scheduled bonuses for the company's senior executives and 6,400 employees across the sprawling corporation. Mr. Geithner last week pressured A.I.G. to cut the $9.6 million going to the top 50 executives in half and tie the rest to performance.

The payment of so much money at a company at the heart of the financial collapse that sent the broader economy into a tailspin almost certainly will fuel a popular backlash against the government's efforts to prop up Wall Street. Past bonuses already have prompted President Obama and Congress to impose tough rules on corporate executive compensation at firms bailed out with taxpayer money.

A.I.G., nearly 80 percent of which is now owned by the government, defended its bonuses, arguing that they were promised last year before the crisis and cannot be legally canceled. In a letter to Mr. Geithner, Edward M. Liddy, the government-appointed chairman of A.I.G., said at least some bonuses were needed to keep the most skilled executives.

We cannot attract and retain the best and the brightest talent to lead and staff the A.I.G. businesses which are now being operated principally on behalf of American taxpayers if employees believe their compensation is subject to continued and arbitrary adjustment by the U.S. Treasury, he wrote Mr. Geithner on Saturday.

Still, Mr. Liddy seemed stung by his talk with Mr. Geithner, calling their conversation last Wednesday a difficult one for me and noting that he receives no bonus himself. "Needless to say, in the current circumstances,

Mr. Liddy wrote I do not like these arrangements and find it distasteful and difficult to recommend to you that we must proceed with them.

An A.I.G. spokeswoman said Saturday that the company had no comment beyond the letter. The bonuses were first reported by The Washington Post.

The senior government official, who was not authorized to speak on the record, said the administration was outraged. "It is unacceptable for Wall Street firms receiving government assistance to hand out million-dollar bonuses, while hard-working Americans bear the burden of this economic crisis," the official said.

Of all the financial institutions that have been propped up by taxpayer dollars, none has received more money than A.I.G. and none has infuriated lawmakers more with practices that policy makers have called reckless.

The bonuses will be paid to executives at A.I.G.'s financial products division, the unit that wrote trillions of dollars' worth of credit-default swaps that protected investors from defaults on bonds backed in many cases by sub prime mortgages.

The bonus plan covers 400 employees, and the bonuses range from as little as $1,000 to as much as $6.5 million. Seven executives at the financial products unit were entitled to receive more than $3 million in bonuses.

Mr. Liddy, whom Federal Reserve and Treasury officials recruited after A.I.G. faltered last September and received its first round of bailout money, said the bonuses and "retention pay" had been agreed to in early 2008 and were for the most part legally required.

The company told the Treasury that there were two categories of bonus payments, with the first to be given to senior executives. The administration official said Mr. Geithner had told A.I.G. to revise them to protect taxpayer dollars and tie future payments to performance.

The second group of bonuses covers some 2008 retention payments from contracts entered into before government involvement in A.I.G. Indeed, in his letter to Mr. Geithner, Mr. Liddy wrote that he had shown the details of the $450 million bonus pool to outside lawyers and been told that A.I.G. had no choice but to follow through with the payment schedule.

The administration official said the Treasury Department did its own legal analysis and concluded that those contracts could not be broken. The official noted that even a provision recently pushed through Congress by Senator Christopher J. Dodd, a Connecticut Democrat, had an exemption for such bonus agreements already in place. But the official said the administration will force A.I.G. to eventually repay the cost of the bonuses to the taxpayers as part of the agreement with the firm, which is being restructured.

A.I.G. did cut other bonuses, Mr. Liddy explained, but those were part of the compensation for people who dealt in other parts of the company and had no direct involvement with the derivatives.

Mr. Liddy wrote that A.I.G. hoped to reduce its retention bonuses for 2009 by 30 percent. He said the top 25 executives at the financial products division had also agreed to reduce their salary for the rest of 2009 to $1.

Ever since it was bailed out by the government last fall, A.I.G. has been defending itself against accusations that it was richly compensating people who caused one of the biggest financial crises in American history.

A.I.G.'s main business is insurance, but the financial products unit sold hundreds of billions of dollars' worth of derivatives, the notorious credit-default swaps that nearly toppled the entire company last fall.

A.I.G. had set up a special bonus pool for the financial products unit early in 2008, before the company's near collapse, when problems stemming from the mortgage crisis were becoming clear and there were concerns that some of the best-informed derivatives specialists might leave. It locked in a total amount, $450 million, for the financial products unit and prepared to pay it in a series of installments, to encourage people to stay.

Only part of the payments had been made by last fall, when A.I.G. nearly collapsed. In documents provided to the Treasury, A.I.G. said it was required to pay about $165 million in bonuses on or before Sunday. That is in addition to $55 million in December.

Under a deal reached last week, A.I.G. agreed that the top 50 executives would get half of the $9.6 million they were supposed to get by March 15. The second half of their bonuses would be paid out in two installments in July and in September. To get those payments, Treasury officials said, A.I.G. would have to show that it had made progress toward its goal of selling off business units and repaying the government.

The financial products unit is now being painstakingly wound down.

AIG and the Big Takeover:

Matt Taibbi on How Wall Street Insiders Are Using the Bailout to Stage a Revolution.

In a new article in Rolling Stone Magazine, journalist Matt Tabbi takes an in-depth look at the story behind AIG. The reality is that the worldwide economic meltdown and the bailout that followed were together a kind of revolution, a coup d'état, writes Taibbi. They cemented and formalized a political trend that has been snowballing for decades: the gradual takeover of the government by a small class of connected insiders, who used money to control elections, buy influence and systematically weaken financial regulations.

Just more of the organized crime syndicate that had been controlling the last administration, Republican party, and other congressional members.

Where are the voices in Congress:

Where are the voices in Congress questioning a military approach in Afghanistan?

A group of Afghan parliamentarians have formed a working group to block the military escalation President Obama approved for Afghanistan 1. After seeing their people lose their lives, homes, loved ones, and livelihoods, they are demanding an end to violence. Who is speaking for them in the US Congress?

Congress needs to exercise real oversight over US strategy in Afghanistan. Let congressional leaders know you are watching US strategy in Afghanistan, and they should be too.

The voices of people in the US and Afghanistan who oppose a military approach are being marginalized in the public debate. For more than seven years, the military approach has failed to bring stability to Afghanistan or defeat terrorism. Al Qaeda was involved in more terrorist attacks in the six years following the invasion of Afghanistan than it had been in the six years before, even if we don't count attacks in Iraq and Afghanistan. 2

The cost of the military approach to Afghans has been unimaginable. The American public does not see the faces of fathers who lose their sons, of wives who can't feed their families after the death of their husbands, of children without homes. It is up to those of us who understand the tragedy of this mistake to bear witness and hold our government accountable.

That is why Peace Action West is partnering with Brave New Foundation in calling for committee chairs Sen. John Kerry and Rep. Howard Berman to hold intensive congressional oversight hearings, with a full exploration of non-military solutions that are more likely to make Americans and Afghans safer.

Become an Afghanistan Witness and tell Congress you will not allow them to ignore the truth about Afghanistan. Join the call for real oversight and accountability.

As an Afghanistan Witness, you'll be the first to hear about breaking news and urgent actions when your help will make a difference. You'll help raise awareness of alternatives to military force that are actually more effective at stopping terrorism. Every voice of opposition is critical right now, and you will help us create a debate when the media and Congress fail to do so.

You and I were there pointing out the failure of a military strategy in Iraq before our government was ready to admit it. We finally saw the beginning of the end of the war in Iraq with President Obama's announcement of his withdrawal plan, and that wouldn't have happened without our tireless efforts. Now we must apply the same tenacity and passion to opposing the occupation of Afghanistan.

Thank you for never being afraid to take a stand.

Obama presses aggressive agenda :

Economic recovery tops the president's list, but health care, science and foreign policy are on an ambitious schedule, too.

For all the whining about rolling back Bush's irresponsible tax cuts, the truth is that Obama's plan cuts taxes for 95% of working Americans. Further, it closes huge tax loopholes for oil companies, hedge funds and corporations that ship jobs overseas so that we can invest in the priorities that will get our economy back on track

The budget that passes Congress has the potential to take our country in a truly new direction -- the kind of change we all worked so hard for. We didn't fight to shy away from the tough long-term decisions Washington has ducked for far too long.

President Obama knows, as you do, that our future strength and prosperity depends on Washington finally taking the hard and smart steps in energy, health care, and education that will make sure America and its families are strong for decades to come.

And while his budget reflects those important values and priorities, the President also understands the government has to cut spending like so many families and businesses are being forced to do now. He invests where we need to and cuts where we must.

In the next few weeks we'll be asking you to do some of the same things we asked of you during the campaign -- talking directly to people in your communities about the President's ideas for long-term prosperity. But first, start with your own pledge of support, and the support of your friends, family, and neighbors:

We know this fight won't be easy. But important battles never are. Together, we have the opportunity to shape our country's future. We believed in the power of people to win an improbable election victory. And we believe in the power of people to drown out the cynics and entrenched interests in Washington to bring lasting, meaningful change we can all be proud we played a role in.

For years, budgets have used accounting tricks to hide the real costs of the wars in Iraq and Afghanistan, the Bush tax cuts, and too many other programs. Obama's budget gets rid of the smokescreens and lays out what America's priorities are, what they cost, and how we're going to pay for them.12

This is the change we voted for. President Obama has done his part, now we need to do ours.

Thanks for all you do.

Daniel, Tanya, Peter, Justin and the rest of the team

Want to support our work? We're entirely funded by our 5 million members—no corporate contributions, no big checks from CEOs. And our tiny staff ensures that small contributions go a long way. Chip in to help. Thanks.

Dear IRS,
I am sorry to inform you that I will not be able to pay taxes owed April 15, but all is not lost. I have paid these taxes: accounts receivable tax, building permit tax, CDL tax, cigarette tax, corporate income tax, dog license tax, federal income tax, unemployment tax, gasoline tax, hunting license tax, fishing license tax, waterfowl stamp tax, inheritance tax, inventory tax, liquor tax, luxury tax, Medicare tax, city, school and county property tax (up33 percent last 4 years), real estate tax, social security tax, road usage tax, toll road tax, state and city sales tax, recreational vehicle tax, state franchise tax, state unemployment tax, telephone federal excise tax, telephone federal state and local surcharge tax, telephone minimum usage surcharge tax, telephone state and local tax, utility tax, vehicle license registration tax, capitol gains tax, lease severance tax, oil and gas assessment tax, Colorado property tax, Texas, Colorado, Wyoming, Oklahoma and New Mexico sales tax, and many more that I can't recall but I have run out of space and money.

When you do not receive my check April 15, just know that it is an honest mistake. Please treat me the same way you treated Congressmen Charles Rangel, Chris Dodd, Barney Frank and ex-Congressman Tom Daschle and, of course, your boss Timothy Geithner. No penalties and no interest.   Have a great day.

Help Iraqi Refugees:

Five million Iraqis have been uprooted by conflict, forced to leave everything behind. They are running out of resources where they have sought refuge. Access to food, heath care, education and other essential services is extremely limited, but they are unlikely and unwilling to go back to Iraq in the foreseeable future.

Conditions for Iraqis to return home safely do not exist. Though the Iraqi government has adequate funds, it lacks the capacity and political will to address humanitarian needs. As a result, militias are doing more to provide aid for internally displaced people, garnering support and recruiting desperate civilians.

Failure to address the long-term needs of displaced Iraqis will have dramatic impacts on security inside Iraq. The U.S. must lead international efforts.

Ensure a safe, voluntary return home when possible;
Pressure Iraq to meet its responsibilities to its own people; and
Increase resettlement for those who can't go home.

Bring ALL the Troops Home Now!
End War and Occupation - Iraq, Afghanistan & Palestine!
Money for Human Needs - NOT War!

Amongst other things, we need to change our thinking and our language. For the US government and the press, every person that takes up arms in any way to protect himself and family, or to drive the occupiers out of his country is a "terrorist" or "insurgent" and probably trained by the often sought, but never found, Al-Qaeda.

If we had enough empathy in this country to realize that most of the violence we see in the Middle East is from people who are, to their own people, patriots! If the tables were turned and we were the occupied country, having our citizens shot and our towns bombed by the invaders, we, too, would be "terrorists" and "insurgents," planting IEDs, cutting throats, sniping, anything to drive the invaders and their Quisling officials out of our country.
So it has been with any occupation. If we cannot learn to sit down and talk these things out; to at least come to a mutual understanding, we shall just go on, spending huge sums to kill each individual patriot until we run out of money.

Afghanistan has been eating foreign armies since the time of Alexander. They are very good at it. Ask the British. Ask the Russians. Afghanistan and Northern Pakistan are tribal areas, linked by blood and clan. They do not recognize the artificial borders set up primarily by the West. A relation killed on one side of the border will be avenged, if necessary, by a relative on the other side.

Every time we hit a village or a house with a half-million dollar Hellfire missile, hoping to kill a guy or two with a gun, we create yet another blood feud with a people who do not forgive or forget. I would not be a Russian or American tourist in either country, even in the 22nd century, for there will always be somebody who will remember.

We could be an agency for good, providing engineers, doctors and builders, but we will accomplish little at the point of a gun. It may already be too late. I watched an interview with some Afghans the other day. Several said, "We don't want your bridges and your schools and hospitals, we want you out of our country, and out of our lives!" I think this is, perhaps, the best solution. Just bring the troops home, then concentrate on healing our own, badly damaged, country.

UNIVERSAL DECLARATION OF HUMAN RIGHTS:

PREAMBLE

Whereas recognition of the inherent dignity and of the equal and inalienable rights of all members of the human family is the foundation of freedom, justice and peace in the world,

Whereas disregard and contempt for human rights have resulted in barbarous acts which have outraged the conscience of mankind, and the advent of a world in which human beings shall enjoy freedom of speech and belief and freedom from fear and want has been proclaimed as the highest aspiration of the common people,

Whereas it is essential, if man is not to be compelled to have recourse, as a last resort, to rebellion against tyranny and oppression, that human rights should be protected by the rule of law,

Whereas it is essential to promote the development of friendly relations between nations,

Whereas the peoples of the United Nations have in the Charter reaffirmed their faith in fundamental human rights, in the dignity and worth of the human person and in the equal rights of men and women and have determined to promote social progress and better standards of life in larger freedom,

Whereas Member States have pledged themselves to achieve, in cooperation with the United Nations, the promotion of universal respect for and observance of human rights and fundamental freedoms,

Whereas a common understanding of these rights and freedoms is of the greatest importance for the full realization of this pledge.

The Case for Single Payer, Universal Health Care For The United States:

Why doesn't the United States have universal health care as a right of citizenship?

The United States is the only industrialized nation that does not guarantee access to health care as a right of citizenship. 28 industrialized nations have single payer universal health care systems, while 1 (Germany) has a multi-payer universal health care system like President Clinton proposed for the United States.

Myth One: The United States has the best health care system in the world.
Fact One: The United States ranks 23rd in infant mortality, down from 12th in 1960 and 21st in 1990
Fact Two: The United States ranks 20th in life expectancy for women down from 1st in 1945 and 13th in 1960
Fact Three: The United States ranks 21st in life expectancy for men down from 1st in 1945 and 17th in 1960.
Fact Four: The United States ranks between 50th and 100th in immunizations depending on the immunization. Overall US is 67th, right behind Botswana
Fact Five: Outcome studies on a variety of diseases, such as coronary artery disease, and renal failure show the United States to rank below Canada and a wide variety of industrialized nations.

Conclusion: The United States ranks poorly relative to other industrialized nations in health care despite having the best trained health care providers and the best medical infrastructure of any industrialized nation
Myth Two: Universal Health Care Would Be Too Expensive
Fact One: The United States spends at least 40% more per capita on health care than any other industrialized country with universal health care

Fact Two: Federal studies by the Congressional Budget Office and the General Accounting office show that single payer universal health care would save 100 to 200 Billion dollars per year despite covering all the uninsured and increasing health care benefits.

Fact Three: State studies by Massachusetts and Connecticut have shown that single payer universal health care would save 1 to 2 Billion dollars per year from the total medical expenses in those states despite covering all the uninsured and increasing health care benefits

Fact Four: The costs of health care in Canada as a % of GNP, which were identical to the United States when Canada changed to a single payer, universal health care system in 1971, have increased at a rate much lower than the United States, despite the US economy being much stronger than Canada's.

Conclusion: Single payer universal health care costs would be lower than the current US system due to lower administrative costs. The United States spends 50 to 100% more on administration than single payer systems. By lowering these administrative costs the United States would have the ability to provide universal health care, without managed care, increase benefits and still save money

Myth Three: Universal Health Care Would Deprive Citizens of Needed Services

Fact One: Studies reveal that citizens in universal health care systems have more doctor visits and more hospital days than in the US

Fact Two: Around 30% of Americans have problem accessing health care due to payment problems or access to care, far more than any other industrialized country. About 17% of our population is without health insurance. About 75% of ill uninsured people have trouble accessing/paying for health care.

Fact Three: Comparisons of Difficulties Accessing Care Are Shown To Be Greater In The US Than Canada

Fact Four: Access to health care is directly related to income and race in the United States. As a result the poor and minorities have poorer health than the wealthy and the whites.

Fact Five: There would be no lines under a universal health care system in the United States because we have about a 30% oversupply of medical equipment and surgeons, whereas demand would increase about 15%

Conclusion: The US denies access to health care based on the ability to pay. Under a universal health care system all would access care. There would be no lines as in other industrialized countries due to the oversupply in our providers and infrastructure, and the willingness/ability of the United States to spend more on health care than other industrialized nations.

Myth Four: Universal Health Care Would Result In Government Control And Intrusion Into Health Care Resulting In Loss Of Freedom Of Choice

Fact One: There would be free choice of health care providers under a single payer universal health care system, unlike our current managed care system in which people are forced to see providers on the insurer's panel to obtain medical benefits

Fact Two: There would be no management of care under a single payer, universal health care system unlike the current managed care system which mandates insurer preapproval for services thus undercutting patient confidentiality and taking health care decisions away from the health care provider and consumer

Fact Three: Although health care providers fees would be set as they are currently in 90% of cases, providers would have a means of negotiating fees unlike the current managed care system in which they are set in corporate board rooms with profits, not patient care, in mind

Fact Four: Taxes, fees and benefits would be decided by the insurer which would be under the control of a diverse board representing consumers, providers, business and government. It would not be a government controlled system, although the government would have to approve the taxes. The system would be run by a public trust, not the government.

Conclusion: Single payer, universal health care administered by a state public health system would be much more democratic and much less intrusive than our current system. Consumers and providers would have a voice in determining benefits, rates and taxes. Problems with free choice, confidentiality and medical decision making would be resolved

Myth Five: Universal Health Care Is Socialized Medicine And Would Be Unacceptable To The Public

Fact One: Single payer universal health care is not socialized medicine. It is health care payment system, not a health care delivery system. Health care providers would be in fee for service practice, and would not be employees of the government, which would be socialized medicine. Single payer health care is not socialized medicine, any more than the public funding of education is socialized education, or the public funding of the defense industry is socialized defense.

Fact Two: Repeated national and state polls have shown that between 60 and 75% of Americans would like a universal health care system (see The Harris Poll #78, October 20, 2005)

Conclusion: Single payer, universal health care is not socialized medicine and would be preferred by the majority of the citizens of this country

Myth Six: The Problems With The US Health Care System Are Being Solved and Are Best Solved By Private Corporate Managed Care Medicine because they are the most efficient

Fact One: Private for profit corporation are the lease efficient deliverer of health care. They spend between 20 and 30% of premiums on administration and profits. The public sector is the most efficient. Medicare spends 3% on administration.

Fact Two: The same procedure in the same hospital the year after conversion from not-for profit to for-profit costs in between 20 to 35% more

Fact Three: Health care costs in the United States grew more in the United States under managed care in 1990 to 1996 than any other industrialized nation with single payer universal health care

Fact Four: The quality of health care in the US has deteriorated under managed care. Access problems have increased. The number of uninsured has dramatically increased (increase of 10 million to 43.4 million from 1989 to 1996, increase of 2.4% from 1989 to 1996- 16% in 1996 and increasing each year).

Fact Five: The level of satisfaction with the US health care system is the lowest of any industrialized nation.

Fact Six: 80% of citizens and 71% of doctors believe that managed care has caused quality of care to be compromised

Conclusion: For profit, managed care can not solve the US health care problems because health care is not a commodity that people shop for, and quality of care must always be compromised when the motivating factor for corporations is to save money through denial of care and decreasing provider costs. In addition managed care has introduced problems of patient confidentiality and disrupted the continuity of care through having limited provider networks.

Overall Answer to the questions why doesn't the US have single payer universal health care when single payer universal health care is the most efficient, most democratic and most equitable means to deliver health care? Why does the United States remain wedded to an inefficient, autocratic and immoral system that makes health care accessible to the wealthy and not the poor when a vast majority of citizens want it to be a right of citizenship?

Conclusion: Corporations are able to buy politicians through our campaign finance system and control the media to convince people that corporate health care is democratic, represents freedom, and is the most efficient system for delivering health care

What you can do about this through your state Green Party

Work to pass a single payer, universal health care bill or referendum in your state. State level bills and referenda will be most effective because a federal health care system might in fact be too bureaucratic, and because it is not politically realistic at this time.

Bills or referendum must be written by and supported by health care providers for the legislature to take them seriously. It is thus imperative to form an alliance with provider groups. The most effective provider group to go through is Physicians For A National Health Program which has chapters in every state (see hand out for partial listing of contact people). A number of states already have organized single payer efforts: Massachusetts, California, Washington, Oregon, New Mexico, and Maryland. Join with them.

A first step is to contact state representatives from PNHP and offer to join with them to write and support a bill bringing single payer, universal health care to your state if this has not already been done. The Connecticut and Massachusetts Bills can be used as models to make this task easier (email us at riverbnd@javanet.com and we will send you copies of the bills). A referendum is another way to go, in which case the California referendum can be used as a model.

A second step is to contact state legislators and find a group who are willing to sponsor such a bill.

A third step is to create a coalition of groups to work together to support and publicize this work, or to try to bring together existing groups to work together on this project. Labor unions, progressive democratic groups, Medicare/Senior Advocacy groups, the Labor Party, the Reform Party, UHCAN, existing health care advocacy groups, and state health care provider groups are all imporatnt to work with and get to join such a coalition. The state medical society and state hospital association are critical to work with in order to get any legislation passed. Try to get them to work with you to design a new model for health care delivery. They will be particularly concerned about who will control the system, and be very mistrustful of government. A public trust model with participation by providers, hospitals, business, the public and government is like to be much more acceptable to them than a pure government system. Emphasize doing away with managed care, and get them to try and work with you to find other ways to control costs (necessary to convince politicians) such as quality assurance standards, which will also protect them from malpractice

A fourth step is to give talks in support of your bill or referendum where ever possible. Senior groups, medical staffs, church groups, high school assemblies, and labor unions are particularly good sources. Excellent materials including slides, a chart book and videos are available through PNHP.

A fifth step is to raise money through fund raisers, contributions and benefits held by entertainers. Benefits are particularly useful in bringing out people who you can inform about single payer, universal health care and your efforts.

A sixth step is to develop media access. The creation of videos that can be shown on local cable access TV stations is very effective. Newspaper articles, letters to the editor, and articles by the press are critical. Radio interviews and radio talk shows are important.

Getting the public to write and call their state representatives in support of a proposed bill is critical, as is coordinating testimony at a public hearing.

Because the data about single payer universal health care are so revealing of the problems with corporate America, and because the US citizenry is so concerned and dissatisfied with our health care system these efforts may yield surprisingly positive results and be helpful in establishing the a party of the people, by the people and for the people.

FOREIGN AID & TRADE:

Developing countries could earn tens of billions of dollars from pollution credits thanks to climate change—and make foreign aid a thing of the past in the process.

Soon, the world will see less snow and ice, as well as more floods, hurricanes, droughts, and heat waves. The world's policymakers have long understood what they must do to avert even worse catastrophes: Reduce the growth of the greenhouse gas emissions that are causing the Earth's temperature to rise.

To succeed, however, policymakers need the cooperation of developing countries, without which there can be no genuine solution to climate change. But rapidly developing countries such as China are finally seeing millions of their citizens climb out of wrenching poverty, and they don't want to see their economic growth jeopardized. Yet they just might change their tune when they realize they could reap a windfall of billions of dollars thanks to global warming.

How? With a truly global "cap-and-trade" system for greenhouse gases. Four main components are necessary. First, the international community must set a sensible cap, a ceiling for global emissions. It would shrink over time to ensure that levels of greenhouse gases in the atmosphere don't accumulate beyond a certain level. Second, all countries would have to participate in full. Third, there's the crucial task of fairly divvying up the carbon cake, the target amount of carbon dioxide each country is allowed to emit. Fourth, there must be a way for every country to sell credits if it pollutes less than it is allowed, or buy credits if it can't meet its target—global emissions trading.

The 1997 Kyoto Protocol, the United Nations' first attempt at a cap-and-trade system, made modest steps toward this solution, but crucially developing countries did not participate fully. They feared that industrialized countries would use Kyoto as an excuse to restrict their economic growth. As a result, no emissions targets were set for developing countries, and in the end only 35 countries in total took on caps to their emissions. The United States, the world's largest emitter of greenhouse gases, was not among them, refusing to sign an agreement that had no quantified targets for China and India. Negotiators could slice through that Gordian Knot if there were a way to safeguard developing countries' desire to develop without ignoring the perils of climate change.

In fact, there is—through fully global emissions trading. Developing countries could earn billions of dollars by joining developed countries in selling emissions credits. How? By following the example of places like the United Kingdom. Under Kyoto, the UK is committed to reducing its emissions of greenhouse gases to 12.5 percent lower than 1990 levels by 2010. If it beats that target—say, by making a 15-percent reduction— then it can sell the surplus emission permits to someone else. Developing countries, however, can't sell surplus permits yet because, under the compromise agreed upon in Kyoto, they have no quantified emissions targets in the first place.

For a "Kyoto II" to work, then, that has to change. Many developing countries have said that they might be prepared to take on quantified emissions caps—if these targets were based not on current emission levels, but countries' populations. That would be more fair, they argue, since everyone enjoys an equal share of the atmosphere. Adopting such an approach immediately would be politically impossible for developed countries, since the average person in the United States, for example, contributes about twenty* times as much to global warming as the average person in India.

But what if a move to equal per-person allocations took place gradually, over a negotiated period of decades, rather than overnight? This could lead to a breakthrough in negotiations, because it would shift the focus of the debate from where it's stuck now (in an abstract back-and-forth between developed and developing countries about fairness) to one crucial variable: the date of convergence, when the "carbon cake" is finally divided on the basis of population.

Over time, emissions trading could even become more significant for the developing world than foreign aid, or replace it altogether. Global aid now totals around $100 billion each year, including debt relief. Those financial flows could quickly become dwarfed by those of emissions trading, even at quite modest prices for carbon dioxide permits. And in fact, under a permit allocation system based on population, the poorest countries would be the biggest beneficiaries.

Emissions trading would thus become a major new source of finance for development, and perhaps the best example of "trade not aid." At the same time, developing countries would have every incentive to invest the proceeds of emission permit sales in renewable energy and clean technology, as it would keep their emissions down and allow them to continue selling permits. Unprecedented? Certainly. But developing countries effectively have a veto here: No one can force them to participate in a global climate deal if they don't think it's fair. The key is to find a solution that demonstrates that a sustainable world can be a profitable one too

RENEWABLE ENERGY:

What is Renewable Energy?

Renewable energy resources are virtually inexhaustible in duration but limited in the amount of energy that is available per unit of time. Renewable energy resources include biomass, hydropower, geothermal, solar, wind, ocean thermal, wave action, and tidal action. (The last three are not discussed in this brochure because there were no commercial operations using these resources in the United States in 2004.) In 1850, about 90% of the energy consumed in the United States was from renewable energy resources. Now the United States is heavily reliant on the non-renewable fossil fuels: coal, natural gas, and oil. In 2004, about 6% of all energy consumed and about 9% of total electricity production was from renewable energy resources.

How Is Renewable Energy Used?

Renewable energy is used for electricity generation, heat in industrial processes, heating and cooling buildings, and transportation fuels. In 2004, electricity generation accounted for about 70% of total renewable energy consumption. The total amount of electricity generated from renewable energy was about 359 billion kilowatthours (kWh), about 9% of total U.S. electricity generation. Industrial process heat and building space heating accounted for 25% of renewable energy use and the remainder was used as vehicle fuels.

In the past, renewable energy has generally been more expensive to use than fossil fuels. Plus, renewable resources are often located remote areas and it is expensive to build powerlines to the cities where they are needed. The use of renewable sources is also limited by the fact that they are not always available (for example, cloudy days reduce solar energy, calm days mean no wind blows to drive wind turbines, droughts reduce water availability to produce hydroelectricity).

The production and use of renewable fuels has grown more quickly in recent years due to higher prices for oil and natural gas, and a number of State and Federal Government incentives, including the Energy Policy Acts of 2002 and 2005. The use of renewable fuels is expected to continue to grow over the next 30 years, although we will still rely on non-renewable fuels to meet most of our energy needs

AMERICA IS CRUMBLING:

The American Society of Civil Engineers has released a Report Card for America's Infrastructure, assigning letter grades for the nation's public infrastructure and environment. The ASCE gave the U.S. an average grade of D, and said it will require more than one trillion dollars and a new national public-private partnership to fix it. The grades were determined by a panel of civil engineering experts who evaluated each category on the basis of condition and performance, capacity, and funding. The worst went to schools, which received an F. The best grade was given to mass transit, which was rated a C. Hazardous waste and roads got a D-; drinking water and dams a D; wastewater a D+; and bridges, solid waste, and aviation a C-. By comparison, when the National Council on Public Works Improvement graded the condition of America's infrastructure in 1988, the overall rating was C.

The nation's public works are public assets. All Americans have a stake in their upkeep and operation, and share in the expense of construction and maintenance. Infrastructure often is paid for through tolls, utility bills, special taxes on gasoline and airline tickets, or other user fees. Since everyone depends on a strong infrastructure, a portion of the cost to maintain it comes from general tax revenues. While some needs are being funded already through Federal, state, and local programs and user fees, the current poor condition of the infrastructure indicates that investment levels are clearly inadequate.

Through the years, the Federal government has continued to shift the financial burden for maintaining the infrastructure to the states. However, voters have been reluctant to support new taxes or bond issues to build desperately needed community schools or water treatment plants.

While many infrastructure problems stem from limited funding at all levels of government, several other factors are involved. As a society, the nation continues merely to patch up outdated and fragmented transportation systems instead of investing in innovative technologies, establishing better links between traditional transportation and mass transit, and encouraging new behaviors. It also focuses efforts on "end-of-the-pipe" solutions--cleaning up the hazardous waste after it has contaminated the environment--instead of reducing it at the source.

To help address some of these issues, the ASCE's research arm, the Civil Engineering Research Foundation, has developed a partnership among industry, government, and the academic community. The Partnership for the Advancement of Infrastructure and Its Renewal is designed to foster and move research innovations into practice, as well as produce longer-lasting solutions to America's infrastructure crisis. The following are among the problems that must be addressed:

ROADS AND BRIDGES

While passenger and commercial travel on highways has increased dramatically in the past 10 years, the U.S. has been seriously under investing in needed road and bridge repairs, even failing to maintain the substandard conditions currently existing. This is a dangerous trend that is affecting highway safety as well as the health of the economy.

Road conditions. More than half of America's urban and rural roadways (59%) are in poor, mediocre, or fair condition, reports the Federal Highway Administration FHwA. Although this is a slight improvement from previous years, conditions remain at substandard levels. The FHwA ranks "poor" those roads in need of immediate improvement. "Mediocre" roads need improvement in the near future to preserve usability; "fair" will likely need improvement; "good" are in decent condition and will not require improvement in the near future; and "very good" have new or almost new pavement.

Road performance. Substandard road and bridge design, pavement conditions, and outdated safety features are a factor in 30% of all fatal highway accidents, according to the FHwA. Personal and commercial highway travel continues to increase at a faster rate than highway capacity, and the nation's roads cannot sufficiently support current or projected travel needs. Between 1970 and 1995, passenger travel nearly doubled in the U.S., and road use is expected to increase by nearly two-thirds in the next 20 years. Growth can be attributed to changes in the labor force, income, makeup of metropolitan areas, and other factors.

More than 70% of peak-hour traffic occurs in congested conditions. The cost to the economy--in wasted time and fuel--in just the 10 most congested urban areas is $34,000,000,000 each year. In addition, poor highway conditions hinder effective transport of goods that help support the American economy.

HOW WILL GOVERNMENT STABILIZE FINANCIAL SECTOR?

Washington will get another chance to prove to Wall Street it means business.

Investors are expecting details on the Treasury Department's plans to fix the financial industry. The questions they want answered: How the government will decide which banks are healthy enough to be saved, how their toxic assets will be priced and how officials will convince private investors to buy them.

President Barack Obama's administration has yet to galvanize confidence on Wall Street. Last November's 11-year trading low of 741.02 for the Standard & Poor's 500 index has not yet been breached — but it could be if the government fails to show the market that its efforts are working and tell them more help is on the way, said Phil Orlando, chief equity market strategist at Federated Investors.

The Center for Public Integrity is standing tall and continuing to report on the issues that matter to you, despite brutal economic conditions that are crippling the rest of the news business. In just a few weeks we will be releasing our long-awaited investigation, Roots of the Global Financial Crisis, an analysis and ranking of the subprime lenders and big bankers who were at the root of the current financial crisis. The package will also probe what government knew of the economic threats posed by predatory lending, and examine why so little was done. You won't want to miss this groundbreaking report.

From our international branch, the International Consortium of Investigative Journalists, comes a story uncovering a gaping hole in the U.S. border with Canada, where cigarette smuggling is rampant and enforcement actions have so far been futile. We are also looking at health care; our recent piece, Painkiller Trial Raises Questions for FDA, Pfizer, illuminated the real story behind a controversial painkiller drug trial that may be putting patients at risk.

On other fronts, our Climate Change Lobby and Coal Ash: The Hidden Story reports have both continued to draw serious attention, not just from the media, but from the Obama Administration as well. Check back on our website often to stay up-to-date on these and other investigations. And don't forget to follow the Center's work on Twitter and become our fan on Facebook.

GLOBAL DRUG BUSINESS:
The ability of the U.S. government to stop illegal drugs is handicapped by the size and power of the international narcotics business. Drug production, smuggling and distribution have exploded into a sophisticated multinational business structure, estimated at $400 billion . Here are reports on this ever-expanding business and first hand accounts from businessmen themselves.

I believe that elements working for the CIA were involved in bringing drugs into the country, said Hector Berrellez, DEA field agent.
I know specifically that some of the CIA contract workers, meaning some of the pilots, in fact were bringing drugs into the U.S. and landing some of these drugs in government air bases. And I know so because I was told by some of these pilots that in fact they had done that.

It is clear from interviews with former D.E.A. agents, CIA officials and former Colonel   that the CIA did not ignore narcotics in Central America. Injecting the United States into a Nicaraguan civil war was hardly an easy sell to Capitol Hill, with nightmares of Vietnam still fresh from the 1970s. Any hint of collusion with the drug trade would be like handing a loaded gun to opponents aiming to kill the effort.
But the degree to which that point was communicated to CIA agents in the field, according to the Hitz investigation, does not inspire confidence.

There was no directorate of operations instruction about how to deal with drug allegations during the whole period of the Contra effort, Hitz said. They were in process. They were working on some kind of guidance. But they never published it in black letter and sent it to the field. In Nicaragua, the Smith-Casey letter basically excused CIA officers from reporting drug trafficking among their contacts. Even when it became clear that narcotics could cast a pall on the effort, the CIA appeared unwilling to react.

As early as 1980, a handbook had been developed with a section instructing CIA officers how to deal with contacts suspected of trafficking drugs. But those regulations were ruled inapplicable to the Contra affair, because they were meant for CIA personnel who were specifically collecting narcotics intelligence -- not the case in Central America. Inexplicably, the handbook wasn't formally published until 15 years later.

In addition, in the mid-1980s, any effort to keep the CIA out of the world of drug trafficking was made more difficult by the decision of its boss, Director Casey, to activate what became known as the "off-the books" operation of Oliver North.
Along with a leading role in the Iran/Contra scandal - in which North helped sell arms to Iran to fund the Contra War - North is also said to have employed air and sea transport companies moonlighting as drugs carriers.

When the Kerry Commission released its report in 1988, the company Frigorificos De Puntarenas was listed as receiving $261,000 in funds from the Nicaraguan Humanitarian Assistance Office, an organization established in 1985 to spend $27 million in congressional humanitarian aid to the Nicaraguan resistance.
Frigorificos' owner, Luis Rodriguez, also operated Ocean Hunter/Mr. Shrimp out of Miami, Florida.

In 1986 the DEA seized 400 pounds of cocaine hidden in yucca addressed to Ocean Hunter. Rodriguez later testified that both companies were used to launder drug money between Costa Rica and Miami.
North has categorically denied that anybody in his operation was trafficking drugs. But in 1987, a co-owner of the shrimp companies pointed the finger at the National Security Council. Moises Nunez told the CIA that he had had a clandestine relationship with the National Security Council since 1985.

If we have a foreign policy that says we're going to oppose the spread of Communism, that's not inconsistent with the (drug) policy, North said in an interview with FRONTLINE. "We're not going to tolerate the flow of drugs into this country. Unfortunately you've got members of Congress up there who want to beat the drum and blame the problem of narcotics in America on the Nicaraguan resistance. And that's just not the case.

He is either misinformed or lying, Winer says. "Oliver North's diaries are filled with references to drug trafficking and people associated with his enterprise drug trafficking--filled with it. Oliver North can say, 'I never hired or worked with any drug traffickers.' His organization did." A good republican before, during, and after.

While the Kerry report listed several companies used by the Nicaraguan Humanitarian Assistance Office that had drug ties, it failed to pass definitive judgement on how much government agencies knew about those ties.

At best, these incidents represent negligence on the part of U.S. government officials responsible for providing support to the Contras, the Hitz report stated. 'At worst, it was a matter of turning a blind eye to the activities of companies who use legitimate activities as a cover for their narcotics trafficking.

If you put aside conspiracy theories of crack peddling, that still leaves the question of why the Agency has repeatedly found itself associated with drug traffickers.

To add to the list of theories and speculations, Fred Hitz has his own. I would call them bureaucratically challenged," Hitz said. "(The CIA) didn't get it done. Having studied the agency over a period of eight years and the bureaucracy that is involved, it grieves me but doesn't surprise me that nobody grasped the nettle and got the right information to the field."

No conspiracy, he said. That's ineptitude. Yes, there are lots of things going on. There is congressional testimony. There are crises in other parts of the world. There are things that are keeping the individuals who write these regulations busy; but that's no excuse. You've got to get to it. Drugs have long played a prominent role in the affairs of the Middle East.

The Middle East is ideally suited to profit from all phases of the drug trade. Climate, geography, and, more recently, politics have combined to make the region an important source and transit point of drugs destined for Europe, the United States, and many of the countries of the Middle East itself. Traditionally, the most important drugs in the Middle East have been opium and marijuana, which provide the raw material for the heroin and hashish that form the staple of the illicit drug trade in the region. Both the opium poppy and marijuana grow easily in many parts of the Middle East and North Africa, and the centuries-old trade routes that crisscross the region give illicit drug producers ready access to the major international drug markets. Although the drug trade is driven largely by the profits inherent in any lucrative criminal activity, in the Middle East it has taken on an important political dimension as rival groups have used enormous drug revenues to pay for the arms necessary to pursue their political ambitions. With a metric ton of heroin worth between $100 million and $600 million, retail, on the streets of the United States, drug sales are an appealing source of immediate, vast revenues for clandestine or criminal activities.

The importance of the Middle East in the international drug trade has varied according to the demand for certain illicit drugs. The taste for drugs is cyclical, alternating between periods of demand for stimulants such as cocaine and amphetamines, and times when the drug-abusing public seeks depressants such as opiates (e.g., morphine, heroin, and other opium derivatives) and hashish. Because the Middle East primarily produces depressants, its importance as a drug source increases when opiates are in demand, as in the 1930s, 1970s, and 1990s.

Opiates

Because Papaver somniferum grows best at higher altitudes, Turkey, Afghanistan, Iran, and more recently Lebanon, have at different times been major sources of heroin and other opiates. In the late 1960s and early 1970s, Turkey gained international notoriety as the principal source of the heroin that fed an epidemic of drug abuse in the United States and Europe. In 1973, as part of an agreement with the United States, Turkey first banned, then allowed only very restricted cultivation of opium poppies for medicinal purposes. This is still the only successful drug crop-control program of its kind, with virtually no leakage into illicit channels.

With Turkey effectively eliminated as a source in the mid-1970s, the center of illicit opiate production shifted eastward to Afghanistan, Lebanon, and, to a lesser extent, Iran. In both Afghanistan and Lebanon, the chaos created by civil war, coupled with the absence of a strong central government and rival combatants' desire for a source of revenue for arms purchases, led to an explosion of opium cultivation. By 1992, Afghanistan had become second only to Myanmar (Burma) in the production of illicit opium. The U.S. government estimated that at the end of 1992, Afghanistan had over 48,000 acres (nearly 19,500 ha) of opium poppy under cultivation, capable of producing 705 tons (640 metric tons) of opium or 70 tons (64 metric tons) of heroin. This would be enough to satisfy estimated heroin needs in the United States six times over and to pump between $6.4 billion and $38.4 billion into the underworld economy. While a large percentage of these opiates is probably consumed by addicts in Afghanistan, Iran, and Pakistan, the remainder flows into the international drug trade through Iran for transshipment to heroin refineries in Turkey and Lebanon. There is also evidence that Afghan opium is flowing northward into new routes opened in central Asia following the collapse of the Soviet Union in 1991.

Although not an opium producer on the scale of Afghanistan, Lebanon is an important country in the international heroin trade. Following Syria's occupation of the Biqa valley in 1976, eastern Lebanon became a center of opium cultivation and heroin refining. The Lebanese government has blamed the Syrian military for the Biqa valley drug trade, which in 1991 had the capacity to produce an estimated 37 tons (34 metric tons) of opium (or 3.7 tons [3.4 metric tons] of heroin) from an estimated nearly 8,400 acres (3,400 ha). Subsequently, a combination of harsh weather and joint Syrian - Lebanese eradication efforts have reduced cultivation to an estimated nearly 1,100 acres (440 ha) in late 1993, though clandestine laboratories may be refining more than 5.5 tons (5 metric tons) a year of heroin from Afghan opium.

Despite Iranian government efforts to ban the opium poppy in 1980, Iran in 1992 was still an important potential source of opium. The U.S. government estimated that nearly 8,650 acres (3,500 ha) of Papaver somniferum were under cultivation at the end of the year. There are indications, however, that Iran's addicts consume most domestic opium production. Iran continues to be a conduit for Afghan and Pakistani opiates moving to Turkey and onward along the Balkan route into Europe.

Hashish:

Although there is cannabis cultivation in nearly every country of the Middle East, only Morocco and Lebanon are significant hashish producers and exporters. Hashish is simple to manufacture, requiring little of the intensive labor and none of the chemicals needed to refine opiates. And while it does not generate profits on the same scale as opiates, hashish production is a multimillion-dollar criminal enterprise. In 1992, Morocco's nearly 74,000 acres (30,000 ha) of cannabis potentially yielded nearly 9,918 tons (9,000 metric tons) of hashish, most of which was destined for Europe. Lebanon, with an estimated nearly 38,800 acres (15,700 ha) of cannabis under cultivation in 1993, potentially had 623 tons (565 metric tons) of hashish available for export. Cannabis may be sold and used legally in many countries so most governments accord cannabis control a relatively low priority. The hashish trade is likely to remain steady therefore, even as the governments of the Middle East intensify efforts to suppress illicit opiates and stimulants.

Illegal Drug Trade:

Great news! The global War on Drugs has been so effective that only 200 million people now use drugs! According to an as-yet-unpublished UN report, despite multi-billion-pound anti-drug measures that have restricted some supplies, the market is as insatiable as ever. What the report didn't mention is at this rate every man, woman, and child on planet earth will be on drugs by Christmas. (Expect some wild New Year's celebrations!)

A second new report, issued by the US State Department, confirms the UN picture of a world using more drugs than ever. Though narcotic use has stabilized in North America, the world's biggest single market, it has boomed in Southeast Asia and Australasia, where use of amphetamine-type stimulants, many manufactured in China, has rocketed. Hmmm ... they have been keeping Australasia a very tight secret haven't they?
South America, Africa, and the Caribbean have also seen serious drug problems emerging. In Europe, though the rapid rise of cocaine use has slowed, an estimated 5.3 per cent of the population used cannabis in the past year and heroin and crack use is still increasing in many regions. Go Drug war! Yay!

This is proof positive that prohibition creates a black market, floods the streets with drugs and churns out crime as fast as you can say would you please hand me my crack pipe, it's under that diaper bag?

Antonio da Costa, director of the UNODC, said global demand reduction measures (like execution, imprisonment, the chopping off of hands) have been "lackluster" and "uninspiring" in recent years. He neglected to point out that the current policies have failed miserably, in every way. Demand, supply, addiction, and abuse are rampant globally. Murder, theft, and money laundering are the norm all over the world.
One of the problems that looms huge is the explosion of amphetamine drugs in the Far East, where their use is reportedly becoming endemic. With America holding the world's largest prison and jail population, the rest of the world can hardly look to the United States for any form of effective leadership on these issues.

The American report says that demand for drugs has increased in three quarters of the some 150 countries surveyed. Consumption levels in some states are surprisingly high--Israel uses 100 tons of pot, 20 tons of hashish, 20 million tabs of ecstasy, four tons of heroin, three tons of cocaine, and hundreds of thousands of LSD blotters annually. Wow, they are really partying down over there!

The result of another failed Bush administration policy, the opium harvest last year was record huge--4,200 tons. "Experts" hope the large harvest will mean that less opium will be planted in future years, as the price goes down from the market glut. However, the cheap price of heroin is already impacting many regions. Thirty countries are reporting a rise in heroin use since 2003, 25 were stable--and only 18 reported a decrease.

So the stark reality is that people are going to use drugs regardless of the penalties and the consequences. It seems like it would behoove society to attempt to educate and regulate to the degree where the harm from all those drugs was reduced. After all, is this about drug use or the harm that is caused by it? Now if you'll excuse me, I must be off to Israel. It's party time!

JOBLESS: 4 states above 10%:

The state-by-state readings come just days after the government reported nationwide unemployment of 8.1%.

As unemployment soared in January, four states' jobless rates climbed higher than 10%, according to federal data released Wednesday.

In January, 49 states and the District of Columbia recorded month-over-month unemployment rate increases, the Labor Department reported. All 50 states and the District of Columbia had higher rates than the previous year.

Non-farm job totals fell in 42 states, increased in 7 states and the District of Columbia, and were unchanged in Vermont.

Only Louisiana's jobless rate decreased. It fell to 5.1%, 0.4 percentage point lower than the previous month. The report also included information for Puerto Rico. The U.S. commonwealth's jobless rate fell 0.5 percentage point from last month, but still stands at a whopping 13%.

The state-by-state unemployment report for January came after the government reported Friday that employers slashed 651,000 jobs across the nation in February and a revised 655,000 jobs in January.

Foreclosures Hit Record Levels:

Only less than half of the year has passed, and the real estate industry has already seen some of the toughest times it has faced in history. A real mortgage crunch has hit the market, causing a significant crisis that has shaken both wall street and the average American citizen. With so many Americans unable to meet their loan payments, more and more individuals are losing their homes to foreclosure, the results of which have risen to record levels.

In April, approximately 243,353 households received a foreclosure notice, which comes close to reaching almost one out of every 519 homes in America. This estimation is in accordance with the FMR, or Foreclosure Market Report, delivered by RealtyTrac, a U.S real estate online marketplace that keeps track of foreclosed properties. The values delivered in the report are up 4% from the month of March, and have surpassed the staggering record number of 239,851 that was set in August of 2007.

James Saccacio, chief executive of RealtyTrac, has commented on the issue, saying that the record set in April is the highest total the company has seen since they began issuing the report back in early 2005.

The measure of foreclosures by RealtyTrac includes auction sales, bank repossessions, and notices of default. Over 54k homes were fully repossessed by lenders and banks, according to the FMR.

The real estate market, which was already saturated to begin with, has seen the negative influence of this recent influx of foreclosed homes, causing the already weakened property values to drop even further. As a result of the plunging value of homes, the amount of money that local government can collect in taxes is vastly reduced, significantly hurting the economy in the process.

All across the nation, the prices of homes have fallen over 7% since the beginning of 2008, reaching the lowest levels of value since the 80s. Corresponding to that value is the number of homes on the real estate market, which has shot up over 3% during the month of April.

Education and Society:

According to "A Nation at Risk", the American education system has declined due to a "rising tide of mediocrity" in our schools. States such as New York have responded to the findings and recommendations of the report by implementing such strategies as the "Regents Action Plan" and the "New Compact for Learning".

In the early 1980's, President Regan ordered a national commission to study our education system. The findings of this commission were that, compared with other industrialized nations, our education system is grossly inadequate in meeting the standards of education that many other countries have developed. At one time, America was the world leader in technology, service, and industry, but overconfidence based on a historical belief in our superiority has caused our nation to fall behind the rapidly growing competitive market in the world with regard to education. The report in some respects is an unfair comparison of our education system, which does not have a national standard for goals, curriculum, or regulations, with other countries that do, but the findings nevertheless reflect the need for change. Our education system at this time is regulated by states which implement their own curriculum, set their own goals and have their own requirements for teacher preparation. Combined with this is the fact that we have lowered our expectations in these areas, thus we are not providing an equal or quality education to all students across the country. The commission findings generated recommendations to improve the content of education and raise the standards of student achievement, particularly in testing, increase the time spent on education and provide incentives to encourage more individuals to enter the field of education as well as improving teacher preparation.

N.Y. State responded to these recommendations by first implementing the Regents Action Plan; an eight year plan designed to raise the standards of education. This plan changed the requirements for graduation by raising the number of credits needed for graduation, raising the number of required core curriculum classes such as social studies, and introduced technology and computer science. The plan also introduced the Regents

Minimum Competency Tests, which requires a student to pass tests in five major categories; math, science, reading, writing, and two areas of social studies. Although the plan achieved many of its goals in raising standards of education in N.Y. State, the general consensus is that we need to continue to improve our education system rather than being satisfied with the achievements we have made thus far.

Therefore, N.Y. adopted "The New Compact for Learning". This plan is based on the principles that all children can learn. The focus of education should be on results and teachers should aim for mastery, not minimum competency. Education should be provided for all children and authority with accountability should be given to educators and success should be rewarded with necessary changes being made to reduce failures. This plan calls for curriculum to be devised in order to meet the needs of students so that they will be fully functional in society upon graduation, rather than just being able to graduate. Districts within the state have been given the authority to devise their own curriculum, but are held accountable by the state so that each district meets the states goals that have been established.

Teachers are encouraged to challenge students to reach their full potential, rather than minimum competency. In this regard, tracking of students is being eliminated so that all students will be challenged, rather than just those who are gifted. Similarly, success should be rewarded with recognition and incentives to further encourage progress for districts, teachers and students while others who are not as accomplished are provided remedial training or resources in order to help them achieve success.

It is difficult to determine whether our country on the whole has responded to the concerns that "A Nation at Risk" presented.

Clearly though, N.Y. State has taken measures over the last ten years to improve its own education system. In many respects the state has accomplished much of what it set out to do, but the need to continue to improve is still present. Certainly, if America is determined to regain its superiority in the world, education, the foundation of our future, needs to be priority number one.

Teachers often develop academic expectations of students based on characteristics that are unrelated to academic progress.

These expectations can affect the way educators present themselves toward the student, causing an alteration in the way our students learn, and thus causing an overall degeneration in the potential growth of the student.

Expectations affect students in many ways, not just academically, but in the form of mental and social deprivation which causes a lack of self-esteem. When educators receive information about students, mostly even before the student walks into their classroom, from past test scores, IEP's, and past teachers, it tends to alter the way we look at the students potential for growth. This foundation of expectation is then transformed on to our method of instruction.

One basic fallout from these expectations is the amount of time educators spend in communicating with students. We tend to speak more directly to students who excel, talking in more matures tone of voice, treating them more like a grown-up than we do to the students who are already labeled underachievers. This can give the student an added incentive to either progress or regress due to the amount of stimulation that they receive.

As educators we tend to take the exceptional students "under our wing". We tend to offer knowledge in situations to help push the good students, in comparison to moving on to the next task for the others. We also tend to critique the work of our god students more positively than the others, offering challenges to the answers they have given.

The most obvious characteristic that educators present to the students is in the area of body language and facial expression. We tend to present ourselves in a more professional manner to our good students, speaking more clearly and with a stronger tone of voice. We tend to stand more upright, in a more powerful stance, than to the slouching effect we give to the underachievers. The head shakes, glancing with our eyes, hand gestures, and posture all contribute to the way we look at certain students based on our first impressions which came before we even knew the student.

One major way we can avoid these pitfalls and eliminate unfair expectations that help produce failure in our students is to restrict the past information on the students to a need to know basis. Instead of telling the teacher how the student did on past examinations, just present them with the curricula that the student must learn during the time they spend in that class. This enables the educator to formulate their own opinions of that student. Also, instead of doing the IEP meetings during the middle of the year, we should wait till the end of the semester to inform the educators of certain aspects of the student instead of giving them all the information earlier in the year.

Finally, it is up to the educator himself to evaluate their own teaching methods to be able to recognize, and change, the way they present themselves to the entire class. To be able to know what we are doing, and how we are doing it, at different times in the day is crucial to the aura we present to the students.

Schools are often blamed for the ills of society, yet society has a major impact on our education system. The problems that schools are facing today are certainly connected to the problems that are society faces, including drugs, violence, and the changing of our family structure. There are many methods that schools have begun to use in order to deal with the problems they are faced with and still offer the best possible education to our youth.

The use of drugs in the general population has become a very serious problem in society and within the school system. There are two aspects to drug use that teachers are having to deal with now.

The first is in trying to teach the new generation of crack babies that are now entering the schools. These students have extremely low attention spans and can be very disruptive in class. Early intervention programs designed to target these children and focus on behavior management within the school setting have been effective in preparing these students for school. Educators have also identified drug use among students as one of the most significant problems that our schools face today. According to the text, the rate of drug use among students has declined in last few years, but recently there has been an increase in alcohol abuse among teenagers. Intervention programs such as APPLE, (a school based rehabilitation facility) have been implemented in many schools with the cooperation of school counselors and community agencies to treat drug using teenagers. Other programs, such as D.A.R.E have been implemented in many elementary schools to provide education about drugs to young students.

Violence, both in society and in the school system has also been identified as a serious problem. The influx of weapons in schools creates a dangerous situation for teachers, administrators and other students. One remedy for this problem has been introduced in many public city schools; the use of metal detectors. While this method is not foolproof it does send the message that violence will not be tolerated in schools and that severe measures will be implemented in order to curb it. Educators are also being trained to identify those students who may be violent and to provide non-violent crisis intervention. It is an undeniable fact that our society has a serious problem concerning violence and that the violence on the streets is certainly connected to the violence in the schools. It seems questionable that even these measures will significantly reduce the problem in schools, but certainly the process of teaching can continue in a less stressful atmosphere by having these measures in place.

Unfortunately, there are other problems such as the changing family structure that do not have such clear cut solutions. Some of the problems that teachers are faced with concerning the family include poverty, single parent homes, abuse and/or neglect and homelessness.

Statistics state that 41% of single, female headed households live below the poverty level and that students who live in single parent homes score lower on achievement tests, particularly boys whose mothers are the head of the household. Obviously, single parent families are a fact in our society today, given the rising rate of divorce and single women having children, and it is true that this change is having a severe effect on students today, but this should not effect the quality of education that is provided, but rather, encourage educators to be more aware of the difficulties these students face in order to adapt their teaching style, as well as the curriculum to reach these students.

Similarly, child abuse and/or neglect has become a major issue in society and schools. It is not clear whether there is a rise in the occurrences of abuse or whether better awareness has increased the statistics, but it cannot be argued that this a significant problem and one that effects those educators who have to help students who are either abused or neglected. Strict regulations concerning the accountability of teachers regarding the reporting of child abuse or neglect are in effect. Teachers are required to be trained on the ability to identify abuse. Community agencies, shelters and child welfare agencies have begun working in conjunction with schools in order to deal with the problem with as little disruption in the student's education as possible.

Homelessness is another major problem in our society. The rate of homeless people has grown significantly since the early 1980's deinstitutionalization movement and more recently due to the rising unemployment rate have led to more families and children being homeless than ever before. This social problem has become a significant problem for educators. Low achievement, which may be in part due to low attendance as a result of a transient lifestyle, physical problems associated with living on the streets and child abuse are all issues that educators are confronted with when working with students who are homeless. Unfortunately, because of the lack of government funds, this problem continues to grow in America. On the other hand, schools have begun to deal with this problem by hiring additional counselors, some who work specifically to coordinate service with shelters in order provide assistance to these families and more precisely to the children. This effort clearly demonstrates that educators are genuinely concerned about providing education to all children.

Clearly our schools and society face the same problems. It has become necessary for all people, not just educators, to be more aware of the problems. Although some intervention programs have been implemented and in some cases are very successful, it is becoming more apparent that these problems are going to continue and will have a direct consequence on our future in this country. Unfortunately, we as a society tend to look for the "quick fix" to our problems without realizing the consequences for the future. Our society need to understand that the schools are not responsible for the cause of these problems or the solutions, but rather, all aspects of society, including schools, are intertwined and need to collectively work together if we are ever to make progress toward resolving these problems in the long run.

Last Gasp for the Israel Lobby:

Is the Israel lobby in Washington an all-powerful force? Or is it, perhaps, running scared?
Judging by the outcome of the Charles W. ("Chas") Freeman affair this week, it might seem as if the Israeli lobby is fearsome indeed. Seen more broadly, however, the controversy over Freeman could be the Israel lobby's Waterloo.

Let's recap. On February 19th, Laura Rozen reported at ForeignPolicy. com that Freeman had been selected by Admiral Dennis Blair, the director of national intelligence, to serve in a key post as chairman of the National Intelligence Council (NIC). The NIC, the official in-house think tank of the intelligence community, takes input from 16 intelligence agencies and produces what are called "national intelligence estimates" on crucial topics of the day as guidance for Washington policymakers. For that job, Freeman boasted a stellar resumé: fluent in Mandarin Chinese, widely experienced in Latin America, Asia, and Africa, a former U.S. ambassador to Saudi Arabia during the first Gulf War, and an ex-assistant secretary of defense during the Reagan administration.

A wry, outspoken iconoclast, Freeman had, however, crossed one of Washington's red lines by virtue of his strong criticism of the U.S.-Israeli relationship. Over the years, he had, in fact, honed a critique of Israel that was both eloquent and powerful. Hours after the Foreign Policy story was posted, Steve Rosen, a former official of the American Israel Public Affairs Committee (AIPAC), launched what would soon become a veritable barrage of criticism of Freeman on his right-wing blog.

Rosen himself has already been indicted by the Department of Justice in an espionage scandal over the transfer of classified information to outside parties involving a colleague at AIPAC, a former official in Donald Rumsfeld's Pentagon, and an official at the Israeli embassy. His blog, Obama Mideast Monitor, is hosted by the Middle East Forum website run by Daniel Pipes, a hard-core, pro-Israeli rightist, whose Middle East Quarterly is, in turn, edited by Michael Rubin of the American Enterprise Institute. Over approximately two weeks, Rosen would post 19 pieces on the Freeman story.

The essence of Rosen's criticism centered on the former ambassador's strongly worded critique of Israel. That was no secret. Freeman had repeatedly denounced many of Israel's policies and Washington's too-close relationship with Jerusalem. The brutal oppression of the Palestinians by the Israeli occupation shows no sign of ending, said Freeman in 2007. American identification with Israel has become total. But Rosen, and those who followed his lead, broadened their attacks to make unfounded or exaggerated claims, taking quotes and emails out of context, and accusing Freeman of being a pro-Arab "lobbyist," of being too closely identified with Saudi Arabia, and of being cavalier about China's treatment of dissidents. They tried to paint the sober, conservative former U.S. official as a wild-eyed radical, an anti-Semite, and a pawn of the Saudi king.

From Rosen's blog, the anti-Freeman vitriol spread to other right-wing, Zionist, and neoconservative blogs, then to the websites of neocons mouthpieces like the New Republic, Commentary, National Review, and the Weekly Standard, which referred to Freeman as a "Saudi puppet." From there, it would spread to the Atlantic and then to the op-ed pages of the Wall Street Journal, where Gabriel Schoenfeld called Freeman a "China-coddling Israel basher," and the Washington Post, where Jonathan Chait of the New Republic labeled Freeman a "fanatic."

Before long, staunch partisans for Israel on Capitol Hill were getting into the act. These would, in the end, include Representative Steve Israel and Senator Charles Schumer, both New York Democrats; a group of Republican House members led by John Boehner of Ohio, the minority leader, and Eric Cantor of Virginia, the Republican Whip; seven Republican members of the Senate Select Committee on Intelligence; and, finally, Senator Joe Lieberman of Connecticut, who engaged in a sharp exchange with Admiral Blair about Freeman at a Senate hearing.

Though Blair strongly defended Freeman, the two men got no support from an anxious White House, which took (politely put) a hands-off approach. Seeing the writing on the wall -- all over the wall, in fact -- Freeman came to the conclusion that, even if he could withstand the storm, his ability to do the job had, in effect, already been torpedoed. Whatever output the National Intelligence Council might produce under his leadership, as Freeman told me in an interview, would instantly be attacked. "Anything that it produced that was politically controversial would immediately be attributed to me as some sort of political deviant, and be discredited," he said.

On March 10th, Freeman bowed out, but not with a whimper. In a letter to friends and colleagues, he launched a defiant, departing counterstrike that may, in fact, have helped to change the very nature of Washington politics. "The tactics of the Israel lobby plumb the depths of dishonor and indecency and include character assassination, selective misquotation, the willful distortion of the record, the fabrication of falsehoods, and an utter disregard for the truth," wrote Freeman.
The aim of this lobby is control of the policy process through the exercise of a veto over the appointment of people who dispute the wisdom of its views.

Freeman put it more metaphorically to me: It was a nice way of, as the Chinese say, killing a chicken to scare the monkeys. By destroying his appointment, Freeman claimed, the Israel lobby hoped to intimidate other critics of Israel and U.S. Middle East policy who might seek jobs in the Obama administration.

On Triumphs, Hysterias, and Mobs

It remains to be seen just how many "monkeys" are trembling. Certainly, the Israel lobby crowed in triumph. Daniel Pipes, for instance, quickly praised Rosen's role in bringing down Freeman:

What you may not know is that Steven J. Rosen of the Middle East Forum was the person who first brought attention to the problematic nature of Freeman's appointment," wrote Pipes. Within hours, the word was out, and three weeks later Freeman has conceded defeat. Only someone with Steve's stature and credibility could have made this happen.

The Zionist Organization of America, a far-right advocacy group that supports Israel, sent out follow-up Action Alerts to its membership, ringing further alarm bells about Freeman as part of a campaign to mobilize public opinion and Congress. Behind the scenes, AIPAC quietly used its considerable clout, especially with friends and allies in the media. And Chuck Schumer, who had trotted over to the White House to talk to Rahm Emanuel, President Obama's chief of staff, later said bluntly:

Charles Freeman was the wrong guy for this position. His statements against Israel were way over the top and severely out of step with the administration. I repeatedly urged the White House to reject him, and I am glad they did the right thing.

Numerous reporters, including Max Blumenthal at the Daily Beast website and Spencer Ackerman of Firedoglake, have effectively documented the role of the Israel lobby, including AIPAC, in sabotaging Freeman's appointment. From their accounts and others, it seems clear that the lobby left its fingerprints all over Freeman's National Intelligence Council corpse. Indeed, Time's Joe Klein described the attack on Freeman as an "assassination, adding that the term lobby doesn't do justice to the methods of the various lobbying groups, individuals, and publications: He was the victim of a mob, not a lobby. The mob was composed primarily of Jewish neoconservatives.

On the other hand, the Washington Post, in a near-hysterical editorial, decided to pretend that the Israel lobby really doesn't exist, accusing Freeman instead of sending out a "crackpot tirade." Huffed the Post, "Mr. Freeman issued a two-page screed on Tuesday in which he described himself as the victim of a shadowy and sinister 'Lobby'... His statement was a grotesque libel."

The Post's case might have been stronger, had it not, just one day earlier, printed an editorial in which it called on Attorney General Eric Holder to exonerate Steve Rosen and drop the espionage case against him. Entitled "Time to Call It Quits, the editorial said:

The matter involves Steven J. Rosen and Keith Weissman, two former officials for the American Israel Public Affairs Committee, or AIPAC... A trial has been scheduled for June in the U.S. District Court for the Eastern District of Virginia. Mr. Holder should pull the plug on this prosecution long before then."

In his interview with me, Freeman noted the propensity members of the Israel lobby have for denying the lobby's existence, even while taking credit for having forced him out and simultaneously claiming that they had nothing to do with it. "We're now at the ludicrous stage where those who boasted of having done it and who described how they did it are now denying that they did it," he said.

Running Scared

The Israel lobby has regularly denied its own existence even as it has long carried on with its work, in stealth as in the bright sunlight. In retrospect, however, l'affaire Freeman may prove a game changer. It has already sparked a new, more intense mainstream focus on the lobby, one that far surpasses the flap that began in March, 2006, over the publication of an essay by John Mearsheimer and Steven Walt in the London Review of Books that was, in 2007, expanded into a book, The Israel Lobby. In fact, one of the sins committed by Freeman, according to his critics, is that an organization he headed, the Middle East Policy Council, published an early version of the Mearsheimer-Walt thesis -- which argued that a powerful, pro-Israel coalition exercises undue influence over American policymakers -- in its journal.

In his blog at Foreign Policy, Walt reacted to Freeman's decision to withdraw by writing:

For all of you out there who may have questioned whether there was a powerful Israel lobby, or who admitted that it existed but didn't think it had much influence, or who thought that the real problem was some supposedly all-powerful 'Saudi lobby,' think again.

What the Freeman affair brought was unwanted, often front-page attention to the lobby. Writers at countless blogs and websites including yours truly, at the Dreyfuss Report dissected or reported on the lobby's assault on Freeman, including Daniel Luban and Jim Lobe at Antiwar. com, Glenn Greenwald in his Salon.com column, M.J. Rosenberg of the Israel Peace Forum, and Phil Weiss at Mondoweiss. Far more striking, however, is that for the first time in memory, both the New York Times and the Washington Post ran page-one stories about the Freeman controversy that specifically used the phrase "Israel lobby," while detailing the charges and countercharges that followed upon Freeman's claim that the lobby did him in.

This new attention to the lobby's work comes at a critical moment, which is why the toppling of Freeman might be its Waterloo.

As a start, right-wing partisans of Israel have grown increasingly anxious about the direction that President Obama intends to take when it comes to U.S. policy toward Israel, the Palestinians, Iran, and the Middle East generally. Despite the way, in the middle of the presidential campaign last June, Obama recited a pro-Israeli catechism in a speech at AIPAC's national conference in Washington, they remain unconvinced that he will prove reliable on their policy concerns. Among other things, they have long been suspicious of his reputed openness to Palestinian points of view.

No less important, while the appointments of Hillary Clinton as his secretary of state and Rahm Emanuel as his chief of staff were reassuring, other appointments were far less so. They were, for instance, concerned by several of Obama's campaign advisers -- and not only Robert Malley of the International Crisis Group and former National Security Adviser Zbigniew Brzezinski, who were quietly eased out of Obamaland early in 2008. An additional source of worry was Daniel Shapiro and Daniel Kurtzer, both Jewish, who served as Obama's top Middle East aides during the campaign and were seen as not sufficiently loyal to the causes favored by hardline, right-wing types.

Since the election, many lobby members have viewed a number of Obama's top appointments, including Shapiro, who's taken the Middle East portfolio at the National Security Council, and Kurtzer, who's in line for a top State Department job, with great unease. Take retired Marine general and now National Security Advisor James L. Jones, who, like Brzezinski, is seen as too sympathetic to the Palestinian point of view and who reputedly wrote a report last year highly critical of Israel's occupation policies; or consider George Mitchell, the U.S. special envoy to the Middle East, who is regarded by many pro-Israeli hawks as far too level-headed and even-handed to be a good mediator; or, to mention one more appointment, Samantha Power, author of A Problem from Hell and now a National Security Council official who has, in the past, made comments sharply critical of Israel.

Of all of these figures, Freeman, because of his record of blunt statements, was the most vulnerable. His appointment looked like low-hanging fruit when it came to launching a concerted, preemptive attack on the administration. As it happens, however, this may prove anything but a moment of strength for the lobby. After all, the recent three-week Israeli assault on Gaza had already generated a barrage of headlines and television images that made Israel look like a bully nation with little regard for Palestinian lives, including those of women and children. According to polls taken in the wake of Gaza, growing numbers of Americans, including many in the Jewish community, have begun to exhibit doubts about Israel's actions, a rare moment when public opinion has begun to tilt against Israel.

Perhaps most important of all, Israel is about to be run by an extremist, ultra right-wing government led by Likud Party leader Bibi Netanyahu, and including the even more extreme party of Avigdor Lieberman, as well as a host of radical-right religious parties. It's an ugly coalition that is guaranteed to clash with the priorities of the Obama White House.

As a result, the arrival of the Netanyahu-Lieberman government is also guaranteed to prove a crisis moment for the Israel lobby. It will present an enormous public-relations problem, akin to the one that faced ad agency Hill & Knowlton during the decades in which it had to defend Philip Morris, the hated cigarette company that repeatedly denied the link between its products and cancer. The Israel lobby knows that it will be difficult to sell cartons of menthol smooth Netanyahu-Lieberman 100s to American consumers.

Indeed, Freeman told me:

The only thing I regret is that in my statement I embraced the term 'Israel lobby.' This isn't really a lobby by, for, or about Israel. It's really, well, I've decided I'm going to call it from now on the Avigdor Lieberman lobby. It's the very right-wing Likud in Israel and its fanatic supporters here. And Avigdor Lieberman is really the guy that they really agree with.

So here's the reality behind the Freeman debacle: Already worried over Team Obama, suffering the after-effects of the Gaza debacle, and about to be burdened with the Netanyahu-Lieberman problem, the Israel lobby is undoubtedly running scared. They succeeded in knocking off Freeman, but the true test of their strength is yet to come.

Obama's Serious About Taking an Axe to Corruption and Waste at the Pentagon:

Of all Barack Obama's promises of reform, perhaps the most audacious is his pledge to "restore honesty, openness, and common sense to Pentagon contracting and procurement." Washington is littered with the open-jawed skeletons of such efforts, and given the historic length of the White House to-do list, some might say taking on the defense establishment smacks of hubris. But a raft of recent statements, directives, and appointments indicate the administration fully intends to chaperone Pentagon shopping trips and hold defense contractors accountable in a way they never have been before.

For good reason, the president doesn't specify exactly which golden-age standards he has in mind for the restoration of honesty and openness. In the half-century since Dwight Eisenhower's farewell warning about an unaccountable "military-industrial complex," not much has changed. (Eisenhower was the last president to Audit Gold reserves and Treasury, no one else would, why?) Countless blue-ribbon commissions, white papers, and special hearings on the Hill have been set up to reform the system. Yet most defense analysts agree the problem is worse than ever. The Government Accountability Office estimates that 40 percent of Pentagon acquisitions come in over cost, the most since records began. Five percent of the military's current base budget of $533 billion is thought to be lost through corruption every year. Other billions are simply unaccounted for in the Pentagon's books, larger versions of those missing unmarked bricks of reconstruction cash we sent to Iraq by the hockey bag.

We're spending more than ever before for less and less, says Winslow Wheeler, a lion among Washington's defense reformers and director of the Straus Military Reform Project at the Center for Defense Information. "It's a meltdown."

Fulfilling a campaign pledge, the president has moved swiftly to address the problem. The White House has put an end to no-bid contracts and instructed the Justice Department to sniff out and prosecute cases of contractor waste and theft. Most important, on March 4, the White House ordered the Office of Management and Budget (OMB) to craft strict new guidelines for overseeing contracts government-wide. In announcing this directive, the president singled out the Department of Defense, putting the Pentagon and its practically in-house contractors on notice that the days of "blank checks" are over.

Echoes of the president's frustration can be heard in Congress, where Carl Levin and John McCain have introduced legislation to increase competition and make it easier to pull the plug on weapons programs that overshoot advertised cost. Meanwhile, at the Defense Department, Robert Gates has been making his own noises about the dawn of a more sober era in what the Pentagon buys and how.

If Gates proves the primary engine of reform at the Pentagon, he won't be alone. Running the Pentagon's acquisition's office will be Ashton Carter, a reform-minded policy scholar and physicist who worked in Clinton's Pentagon on non-proliferation issues. As the department's weapons czar, Carter will preside over all meetings between Pentagon officials and contractors. He will decide, in consultation with the Defense Secretary and the White House, which weapons to buy, cut back, and kill. While some defense watchers say Carter lacks the acquisition experience and bureaucratic dog-fighting skills necessary to face down the defense executives, lobbyists, and generals who will be defending some $400 billion in business for contracted goods and services -- "They'll view him as a plaything," says one former employee of a major defense contractor -- others say he may prove a tiger.

It's true Ash Carter doesn't have a lot of acquisition experience, but there are those who think he can be pretty tough," says Barry Watts, a senior fellow at the Center for Strategic Budget Assessment. "We'll have to see how successful he can be in changing the system rather than being run over by it.

bureaucratically weak, says Travis Sharp, an analyst at the Center for Arms Control and Non-Proliferation. "This time around he still has great ideas and a clear view of where the Pentagon needs to go strategically. I think he is up to it, but he'll be pitted against powerful interests in the private sector and on Capitol Hill. He needs allies."

Not all the faces at Obama's Pentagon are so fresh, of course. Many defense watchers and reform advocates remain confused and disappointed that Obama tapped William Lynn, a former Raytheon lobbyist, for number two at the Pentagon. Democrats are willing to trust the president, however, and within the Progressive Caucus only Claire McCaskill (D-MO) opposed the nomination.

Then there is Steve Kosiak, who holds the national security portfolio at OMB. Before joining the government, Kosiak directed budget studies at the Center for Strategic and Budgetary Assessments (CBSA), an independent think tank that frequently produces reports critical of Pentagon planning and 10 and 11-digit weapons programs. Kosiak is known as a liberal and a reformer who cut his teeth under CSBA founder Gordon Adams, another liberal critic of excessive defense spending who served under Clinton in the same role at OMB. Kosiak has been especially critical of futuristic space-weapons programs. In a 2007 report he authored for CSBA, he threw cold water on industry claims that space-weapons were necessary for the country's defense. Kosiak also urged decisions on such weapons be weighed carefully against their potential arms race implications.

It's becoming clear that Obama intends to use [Kosiak and others at] OMB as his primary agents for change," says Wheeler, of the Center for Defense Information. The Pentagon cannot reform itself on its own."

But the White House appears have an ally in Defense Secretary Robert Gates, a career public servant on his last go-around. Last month, Gates told Defense News that the military budget to be released in April will "realize cost efficiencies [and] reassess all weapons programs -- especially those with serious execution issues." In the January/February issue of Foreign Affairs, Gates criticized "ever more baroque" big-ticket weapons systems "that as have become ever more costly, are taking longer to build and are being fielded in ever dwindling quantities."

Next month's budget will see cuts to at least a few of the "baroque" weapons systems that have experienced epic cost overruns in recent years. Among the programs being watched closely are the F-22 Raptor fighter jet, the DDG-1000 destroyer, the Expeditionary Fighting Vehicle, mid-course missile defense, and the services-wide modernization program known as Future Combat Systems. Some combination of these will likely suffer from the "hard choices" Gates says will define Obama's defense budget in 2010 and beyond.

These "hard choices" alluded to by Gates aren't just a result of Congressional or White House outrage over cost overruns and corruption. They are being forced by a quiet and growing tension in the military between people and machines. The main driver of defense budget growth isn't new fighter jets or bloated boondoggles like missile defense. Rather, it's the growing costs of training, equipping, paying, and insuring increasing numbers of U.S. servicemen and women. Nearly sixty percent of the defense budget currently goes to costs related to basic personnel, operations, and maintenance. In ten years, the number is expected to touch 70 percent. "It is an accurate statement that our personnel costs are rising every year and consume a larger percentage of the budget," Gates recently told Defense News. Health care costs in particular, he said, are "increasing at what I would call almost an alarming rate."

Obama has no intention of cutting defense spending in this area. The president's first military budget provides a 2.9 percent pay raise for soldiers and accelerates planned increases in the size of the Army and Marine Corps. "These personnel costs will consume much more than the $9 billion inflation-adjusted budget growth the administration is seeking," notes Travis Sharp, of the Center for Arms Control and Non-Proliferation. "It is inevitable that the procurement and R&D accounts will be cut, because cutting the personnel account is political suicide and cutting the operations and maintenance account is impossible when there are two wars going on."

The question, then, is how best to rationalize procurement and reign in weapons system costs. There are two main schools of thought. One focuses on the process of how we buy weapons; the other on what we buy.

The first theory holds that if strict guidelines and timetables are enforced, boondoggles will be avoided and corruption eliminated. This approach is reflected in the Levin-McCain legislation, forthcoming OMB guidelines, and Obama's pledge to expand the officer contracting corps.

How we buy it is key, says Rudy deLeon, senior vice president of national security and international policy at the Center for American Progress. "The contracting side of the process needs to be greatly strengthened. The technology folks tell us what is possible, but the contracting guys actually obligate what we have to pay for. During the last eight years, the Bush Administration budgets reduced the career civilian workforce, that possess essential contracting expertise. That was a huge loss going out the door.

Others think the wings of the Pentagon's imagination are more dangerous than the lack of contracting oversight. These critics hold that timetables and cost limits will always be broken and revised once high-tech production pipes are opened. The most important thing, they say, is to stop shooting for the military moon. "The problem is not the way we contract, it's what we contract," says Benjamin Friedman, Research Fellow in Defense and Homeland Security Studies at the Cato Institute. "The trouble is we want several technological miracles in each new platform. It's not sustainable."

We can't fix [the Pentagon system] because we want crazy things, writes Harvey Sapolsky, professor of Public Policy and Organization Emeritus at MIT, in a February essay in Defense News. Sapolosky argues that until weapons programs become more realistic, the charade of yet another round of acquisition reform should be skipped altogether. "Changing the rules every time we change administrations or secretaries is a colossal waste of effort, forcing everyone involved to learn a new manual, another set of acronyms and a revised timetable for required approvals.

This growing debate over how best to scale back the most expensive next-generation programs (a debate that will increase with the return of deficit awareness) has not surprisingly led the defense industry to mount a counterattack. Industry's response to the threat to its most expensive programs is to paint defense spending as a crucial economic stimulant during a recession, providing jobs and keeping money pumping through the system via vast nationwide webs of contractors and subcontractors. Whereas these defense firms once posed as patriotic defenders of the American people, they now pose as patriotic employers of the American people. Lockheed Martin recently launched an economics-based national campaign in support of its threatened F-22 Raptor program, on which the Air Force has already spent more than $62 billion for less than 200 planes. The planes do not even appear in the ads.

While such arguments may be tempting for members of Congress with defense industries in their districts and states, the idea that defense dollars equal effective job creation is open to debate, at best. A 2007 study conducted by researchers at the University of Massachusetts concluded that $1 billion of education spending generates as many as twice the number of jobs as military spending. Spending on health care, mass transit, and infrastructure, meanwhile, creates jobs at a lower average salary than military spending, but creates substantially more of them.

But even a dramatic scaling back of the Pentagon's favorite next-generation programs won't free up much money for other kinds of more socially productive economic stimulus programs. Nor will it reduce military budgets on the horizon below the current mind-boggling $500 billion-plus ($700b if you include the war supplemental). Defense budgets will remain high due to rising personnel costs, two wars, and the maintenance of bases around the world. Still, getting the defense contracting process under control is worth doing for a raft of other moral, economic, and national security reasons. It would also be deeply satisfying to see the Pentagon to do like the bumper sticker says and finally hold that bake sale to pay for weapons that come in over cost.

On this front, can the Obama administration succeed where so many others have failed?

Only with the support of you and me!

TAX EXEMPTIONS SHOULD END:

Tax exemption is unfair and needs to end totally. It clearly is said that we should pay our taxes. Why should anyone's stocks, bonds, and real estate be tax exempt.

Charity is to be for the poor, but they rarely see it. Only 10 percent and less ever reaches the needy. But wealth has been made by a large number of greedy persons from contributions. Talk about a fraud system with no audits

Though the measure is rarely enforced, the political activism of some conservative Christians over the past two decades has caused religious and political liberals to demand that the tax-exempt status of some conservative ministers be revoked. Fact being that all should be revoked.

Any way you slice it, this is a government subsidy of religion. People who may not share a particular faith, or any faith, are thus forced to contribute to ideas with which they might disagree. Thomas Jefferson said of such a practice: "Almighty God has created the mind free. ... to compel a man to furnish contributions of money for the propagation of opinions which he disbelieves and abhors is sinful and tyrannical."

Churches may now hold weeknight political forums at which candidates may speak and answer questions. They are prohibited, however, from endorsing candidates from the pulpit, or actively lobbying for or against legislation. We all know the real reality. We would not be in the serious situation we are in today if it were not for the lobbying and complete support for the actions of the Republican Party, Israel, and AIPAC.

There are options to correcting this imbalance in church-state relations.

Most effective is for churches and other nonprofits that are engage in political discourse and legislative activism should give up their tax exemptions so that government will have no controlling authority over them.

 This would be the preference to most because it offers them unfettered opportunity to influence and shape government according to their own beliefs without the fear or favor of government leaders who might support their views today, but after a future election, oppose them.

Exactly what the Republican Party has done for decades. When churches become "accepted" and appendages of political parties and politicians they tend to depart from their primary obligations and opportunities and become identified with earthly causes and political kingdom-building.

The mystical exploitation of religion has created a hierarchy of sanctimonious pedagogues who prosper in an environment free of obligation to the society from which they profit immensely. There is no such thing as a non-profit religion. If there were non-profit religions, most established religions would not exist.

If a mystical organization cannot prosper or survive because of taxation, it must not have a message or purpose worth sustaining, nor the ability to communicate a concept that appeals to the public. If it requires exemption from taxation as the only way it can exist, then it is a religion based on a superficial concept of Biblical nonsense that eventually the public will ignore.

The scheming and manipulation of the frenzied, right wing religious fundamentalists, has proven that religion untaxed, is more dangerous to Liberty than taxation of the same. Why should an institution founded on fantasy and myth, be exonerated from taxation while existing in a society that supports the infrastructure and services that make it possible for that religion to succeed? My freedom, yours, and every other individual that exists in this society, is threatened by the immense influence of organized religion in its massive appeal to legislate laws favorable to its establishment. We, unlike the religionists, do not as individuals, have the use of untaxed funds or Christianized Coalitions that exist to exercise leverage over politicians.

What is Democratic, what is justifiable in allowing the churches the extraordinary freedom to exist exempt from taxation??? Especially when the exempted religions pursue as their objective, the influence of legislation favorable to their continued material advancement. The survival of organized revealed religion is dependent on not only the generosity of its members, but also from a government that is sympathetic to the continued domination of mystical authority in the affairs of state and society. Witness George Bush receiving the blessing from his religious minister for the carpet bombing and resulting mass murder of Iraqi civilians during the Desert Storm exercise in ignorance.

The established religions have prospered in an environment that is maintained through the taxation of others for such simple things as street upkeep, courts of law, police and fire protection, or any of the many other services that the public pays for. It is we the people, who are assuring that religious associations can perform their functions, while they are exempted from the same obligation. They have been granted an exclusion, that is based on the erroneous concept, that religion is a non-profit enterprise. Anyone who believes religion is not profitable and exists solely as a distributor of myth and magic, has not looked recently at the vast resources and property that churches have acquired as non-profit organizations.

The fact Christian religious leaders accept, and even court, the tax-exemption illustrates without question the non-altuistic, greedy and hypocritical nature which permeates Christianity. Not paying your fair share of anything, including taxes, reveals a non-altruistic and greedy streak. That's exactly what you would think of someone in a group of friends who all go on an outing and all chip-in to pay for expenses with the exception of one individual. And that selfish person is one of the very wealthiest people in the group! It will only be a matter of time until the others catch on and refuse to allow the unfairness.

Christian leaders add the ingredient of hypocrisy to themselves and their mythology by pretending to be followers of Jesus who allegedly believed religions SHOULD pay taxes to existing governments by saying, according to Luke 20:25, "Render to Caesar what is Caesar's, and to God what is God's." According to this quote from their holy book, their god would be against tax-exemptions for his followers. As Thomas Paine wrote, "... the Church has set up a system of religion very contradictory to the character of the person whose name it bears. It has set up a religion of pomp and of revenue, in pretended imitation of a person whose life was humility and poverty."

The religions of this nation do not contribute, in any way, to my freedom, your Liberty, or the future of civilization. Freed of taxation they exist exclusively as a hierarchy whose interest is the exploitation of others!

IS IT NOT TIME THAT WE THE PUBLIC DEMAND THAT THE RELIGIONS OF THIS NATION PAY FOR THEIR PARTICIPATION IN SOCIETY??? Is it not the proper time to cease characterizing religious institutions as a privileged ideology that is more important than other philosophies and concepts?

Why should the labor of a person working eight hours a day be taxed, while a preacher is allowed to avoid taxation in many areas? Why should there be a tax for the general public, but not for those engaged in the production (or fabrication) of a religious ideology? Is the enterprise of corporate religion any better or more useful to society than an individual who thinks about existence from a philosophical and rational perspective? I think not. There is no such thing as an aristocracy of thought or complete agreement on any conception. Religion in all its many forms, does not have the exclusive answers to the complexity of existence. Its reliance on mystical incomprehension and the miraculous is rooted in the dreams and desires of primitive man.

Taxation of religion is based on fairness and justice. It is a notification to those who represent corporate religion that they are not a special institution or a favored aristocracy. It is telling them they do have an obligation to support society in the form of taxation. Particularly, as the Christian Coalition is doing, using the millions of dollars saved from taxes to pump into the campaigns of politicians who agreed to spread their brand of bigotry and superstition.

NOW! We all face deficits in the federal budget, every state budget, local budgets, a hugh 12 Trillion national debt. That requires that we all should share in its being resolved.

William H. Rehnquist spoke for the court:

Tax exemption for Church property is a clear violation of the establishment clause of the First Amendment. It is a form of subsidy; the Tenth Circuit Court addressed and held that "tax exemption is a privilege, a matter of grace rather than a right."

We tax payers demand that Churches pay their "Fair-Share"...

The Israeli military ordered seven Palestinian families to evacuate their homes and farm buildings within 48 hours on Tuesday.
All of the structures, all southeast of the West Bank city of Nablus, are slated for demolition.
According to Jad'an Qasim, chair of the Al-Falah Society, Israeli authorities decided to demolish the homes and sheds in the Getit area near the Israeli settlement of Mekhora. Families received notices to evacuate their properties within 48 hours, Qasim explained.
He identified owners of the properties to be demolished as Zayd Bani Minna, Khalil Bani Jabir, Jamil Bani Jabir, Ghallab Hammad, Wasif Hammad, Muhammad Hammad, and Abdullah Bani Jabir.
Qasim appealed to the Palestinian Authority and international organizations to intervene and prevent the demolitions.
The effort marks the third mass-demolition announcement in two months, after Israeli authorities warned residents of Al-Baqa⊠¡½a in south Hebron and Silwan in East Jerusalem that their homes would be destroyed so a settlement can be expanded and park can be built on the areas. Forty will be rendered homeless in Al-Baqa⊠¡½a and 1,500 in Silwan.
Under the 1995 Oslo II Accords, Israel was given rights to 75 to 80% of the water supply from the Western, North-eastern and Eastern Aquifers that straddle the Green Line. At the time, the estimated potential of the aquifers was 679 million cubic meters per year. Israel was supposed

to take about 540 million cu.m. but in fact has been extracting 871 million.

Following Iranian President Ahmadinejad`s controversial Geneva speech in which he called Israel "the most cruel and racist of regimes", Palestinian civil society groups are less than enthusiastic that Tehran`s municipality is engaging Veolia and Alstom for its transportation system - the same French companies involved in building the "Jerusalem Light Rail" - connecting the "Jewish neighborhoods" in unilaterally annexed East Jerusalem.

"The best response to Ahmadinejad`s inflammatory rhetoric is to stay in Geneva and rebut it" said Juliette de Rivero, Geneva advocacy director at Human Rights Watch. The draft document due to be adopted contains no reference to Israel or the Middle East, while reaffirming the tragedy of the Holocaust and condemning anti-Semitism. However, one-sided reports in the Israeli media give the impression of a conference of anti-semites and Holocaust deniers.

-"anywhere from 35 percent to 60 percent of the agriculture industry was destroyed by Israel`s attacks on Gaza, much of it not useable again due to the damage. Even before the attacks, Gaza`s farming sector had been seriously devastated by the crippling siege on Gaza. Whereas Gaza had been producing half of its agricultural needs, the combination of siege and warfare on Gaza has led to the "destruction of all means of life," including destroyed farmland along with hundreds of greenhouses, hundreds of wells and water pumps, and farming equipment. "

-"anywhere from 35 percent to 60 percent of the agriculture industry was destroyed by Israel`s attacks on Gaza, much of it not useable again due to the damage. Even before the attacks, Gaza`s farming sector had been seriously devastated by the crippling siege on Gaza. Whereas Gaza had been producing half of its agricultural needs, the combination of siege and warfare on Gaza has led to the "destruction of all means of life," including destroyed farmland along with hundreds of greenhouses, hundreds of wells and water pumps, and farming equipment. " 7/4/2009

Prevention of medical assistance from the trapped and the wounded, severe difficulties to emergency medical evacuation, attacks on medical personnel and medical facilties, and de facto prevention from the chronically ill and gravely wounded referral to medical care outside Gaza. "We call for an outside independent body to investigate the events" say representatives of Physicians for Human Rights-Israel.

IDF troops ordered the boy to walk in front of soldiers being fired on in the Gaza neighborhood of Tel al-Hawa and enter buildings before them, said the UN secretary-general`s envoy for protecting children in armed conflict. This is but one of the verified human rights atrocities included in the 43-page UN report published Monday.

" The soldier was quoted as saying that the rabbis had "brought in a lot of booklets and articles," adding, "their message was very clear: We are the Jewish people, we came to this land by a miracle. God brought us back to this land, and now we need to fight to expel the non-Jews who are interfering with our conquest of this holy land."

Of course at this time it is the DEVIL'S will.

The only time I have agreed with Pat Buchanan was when he said, "Capitol Hill is Israeli -occupied territory."

Our government covers up the genocide Israel is conducting against the Palestinians. It is s small step from there to start covering up the crimes of our government.

Israel benefits from a fascist government in this country so they can continue to control our foreign policy without any hindrance from we the people.

Our only hope to gain respect from the rest of the world is to free our government from Israel's control.

A good start would be to vote against any candidate who gets money from the Israel Lobby.

The majority of our "representatives" get AIPAC money just to curry favor with them. The real work of controlling our elections by International Judaism is done by directing money support to the one the Jews wish to win in a particular contest - as much as is needed and without limit.

The contributions are coordinated by AIPAC but come from many-many headless Jewish Political Action Committees so that they can subvert our laws limiting contributions from single PAC's.

There is no hope to end this domination of our once proud nation as we simply belong to International Judaism - TOTALLY. the whole world knows that and even our elected 'representatives' know it. 'Only' the vast majority of the American people are in the dark about it.

When I hear anyone wondering just why a country which considers itself a democracy allows itself to be completely controlled by a political party consisting of only 1.7 percent of the population I will see a spark of hope but even then it would take at least decades to grow that spark into a flame.

What the US knew and chose to forget in 1948 and why it matters in 2009:

The PR war being waged by Israel over coverage of its invasion of Gaza is a critical part of maintaining the US public, if not the US government, in a state of maximal ignorance and above all, indifference, to the meaning of what is taking place in Gaza.

There is nothing new about such PR efforts. directed at the U.S. with the tacit understanding that Washington's support is critical to Israel's permanent war against the Palestinians. From Washington's perspective, irrespective of the administration in power, Tel Aviv has played a critical role in the protection of US interests in the Middle East, with the tacit collaboration of Washington's reactionary Arab allies. In this context, the fate of the 1.5 million residents of Gaza, as that of Palestinians in the West Bank, is and has long been, entirely expendable. Whether it is the PLO, Fatah, Hamas, or others who have operated in the ranks of Palestinian politics, the view from Washington has been consistent and compatible with that of Israel. Thus, to the extent that Palestinians are perceived as resistant to US or Israeli policy, they are considered suspect, and in the case of organized parties or movements, intolerable, as in the case of Hamas and the prospect of its survival and influence beyond Gaza. But the PR war being waged over Israel's crushing campaign in Gaza is directed at another front, a popular front whose support

Washington has also coveted and corrupted in the conduct of its Middle East policies. The systematic deception concerning US policy in Iraq put over on the US public, or at least a substantial part of it, is by now well known. The same cannot be said about US policy on Israel/Palestine, a well protected enterprise that persists with great effort. Hence the importance of the Israeli PR war to make sure that the American public remains immune to the latest phase in the war against Palestine, that it remain blind and deaf and above all, distant and detached from the quaking of that earth.

The control of such information in the age of the internet, however, has become virtually impossible. Graphic evidence of what this total war has meant for the Gaza 'strip' that is stripped of any means of survival, defies the ban on knowing. The wordless images of death at the hands of weapons of mass destruction are no longer hidden. Nor is the defiant violation of law, whether national or international kept behind raps. On the contrary, its very openness is an invitation to complicity, or an incitement to rejection borne of an intolerable revulsion as Gaza has come to evoke Guernica, Hiroshima, the Warsaw Ghetto, the forbidden references now current.

Many have pointed out that the Israeli invasion of Gaza bears a highly disturbing resemblance to the massive expulsion of Palestinians in 1948. Some 700,000-800,000 people were dispossessed from their homes as a result of policies pursued by the military forces of what became the state of Israel in May 1948. US policymakers then were fully aware of the origins and likely consequences of what became the Palestine refugee problem. Their responses are part of the documentary record that is, unfortunately, little known today. Yet however significant the major regional and international changes that have occurred in the intervening years, there is an undeniable connection between the traumatic developments of that period and those taking place in the West Bank and, notoriously, in Gaza today. That US officials were fully apprised of the origins of the Palestine refugee problem remains important, that they chose to set it aside and to reward the emergent Israeli state for its ability to violate border agreements and expel the native population of Palestine without incurring effective regional or international challenge, was indicative of Washington's calculations. Those went considerably beyond Palestine.

In 1948 as now, Washington concluded that it had a stake in the outcome of the Palestinian struggle that was inseparable from its interests in the region. It was not Hamas that Washington worried about in 1948, but the prospect of an independent Palestinian state as envisioned in the 1947 UN Partition Plan. Therein lies their preference for the enhanced role of Transjordan in taking over what remained of Palestine, which was the new state of Israel's preferred policy as well.

There was no question then about what would later be described as the demographic transformation of Palestine in the period extending from the UN Partition Resolution of November 29, 1947 to Israel's declaration of independence on May 14, 1948 and continuing through the 1949 armistice agreements. Israel's expansion and consolidation of territory beyond that allotted by the UN Partition Plan elicited opposition in Palestine and beyond, offending British officials and some among their US colleagues. But it quickly became clear that Washington was prepared to legitimize Israel's expansion and support its admission to the UN and then, as now, to accept its resistance to final settlement, lest that involve unacceptable compromise.

US officials were also well aware of the military inferiority of Palestinian and Arab forces as compared to those of the Hagana, the Irgun and the Stern Gang in 1948. US officials, moreover, were witness to the flight and expulsion of Palestinians which they duly recorded in their cables to Washington.

At 5pm on April 13, 1948, the US Consul at Jerusalem (Wasson) cabled the US Secretary of State with the following confidential message:

"Early morning April 9 combined force Irgun and Stern Gang numbering over 100 attacked Arab village, Deir Yasin, several miles west Jerusalem. Attackers killed 250 persons of whom half, by their own admission to

American correspondents, were women and children. Attack carried out in connection battle now still in progress between Arabs Jews on roads leading to Jerusalem from Tel Aviv."[1]

"We believe," continued Wasson, "chance for cease-fire and truce increasingly remote. With growing criticism in Irgun and Stern Gang circles over Haganah leadership further attacks this nature can be expected and Arabs will react violently."

At the end of April it was Haifa, where the mass exodus had begun the previous winter. This time it was Aubrey Lippincott, US Consul at Haifa, who reported on the continued flight and expulsion of Arabs, describing "Arab areas now being evacuated after Arabs refuse meet Haganah truce team which reportedly call for complete surrender arms, equipment, all food supplied, deportation 'foreign' Arabs, and surrender to Jews of all former Nazis."[2] And as Lippincott continued, "Arab families west of Haifa with two thousand women and children reported fled to Acre by sea.... Haifa now undoubtedly completely Jew controlled...." Lippincott continued: "Arab leaders and men proved poor and totally inadequate deal with forces. Survivors claim British prevented seven hundred reinforcements from entering city during battle also claim Abdullah promised help which British also stopped. Arab forces entirely dispersed. Leaders reportedly left before battle occurred." As to the residents of Haifa who remained, they were obliged to acquire identity cards and "must swear allegiance to Israel state," Lippincott reported.

In June, the US consul reported that he had learned from the Honorary Spanish Vice Consul who was also a US citizen: "1. All Arabs who remained Haifa being thoroughly screened by Jewish authorities, required obtain identity cards and must swear allegiance to Israel state. 2. Arabs who return Haifa are considered illegals. Of these Jews are permitting only those to remain whom they consider satisfactory after thorough investigation. These also required take oath allegiance Jewish state. Result is remaining Arabs determined leave."[3] The Honorary Vice Consul of Spain was assisting in departures.

On May 13, the eve of Israel's declaration of independence, it was the turn of Jaffa. This time the account of what occurred was transmitted through the US Minister in Beirut, Lowell C. Pinkerton. In April 1949 he submitted a package containing a long Memorandum to the US Government written by the representatives of the Jaffa and District Inhabitants Council exiled in Beirut.

What did Pinkerton make of his submission? He surely read the Memorandum whose opening paragraph was utterly straightforward:

"First we would draw the attention of the Government of the United States to the following important fact: namely, that the conflict did not originally include or involve such a question as the return of refugees; the population itself never envisaged such a possibility. On the one hand, a large number of people did not leave their homes voluntarily, but were expelled by order of the Jewish commanders when they entered their towns and villages (Ramleh and Lydda), and were prevented from taking any of their belongings with them. On the other hand, the conditions which prevailed shortly before the termination of the Mandate rendered it impossible for a large section of the people to remain in homes and lands. For, that would have meant the destruction of a large number of them, since they did not possess arms with which to defend themselves. The majority of them believed that the matter would be settled politically, not imagining for a moment that things would reach the stage of open and general war. They, as law-abiding civilians, had therefore failed to equip themselves with arms and ammunition even for self-defense. Many, too, placing their trust in the United Nations could not believe they would be left defenceless and helpless against attack. But all of a sudden, the people were faced with imminent danger to their lives and property, and they had no alternative but to take the drastic step of fleeing for the nearest refuge. Most of them made for the neighboring countries, where they found a sympathetic welcome as refugees. But legally speaking, they were (and still are) considered as aliens in these countries, and all the laws and rules that apply to foreigners applied to them as Palestinians."

But Pinkerton also had before him a copy of the surrender agreement dated May 13, 1948, that was signed by the Emergency Committee of Jaffa, which opened with the following warning: "Any shot fired at a Jewish area or at a Jew or at any member of the Hagana, or any resistance to them, will be sufficient reason for the Hagana to open fire at the Offender."[4] And then there was directive number 4:

"All males in the area defined in the Agreement will concentrate in the area between Feisal Street, Al Mukhtar Street, Al Hulwa Street and the Sea until every body has identified himself under arrangements, the particulars of which will be notified later.

"During this time, any male found outside this area will be severely punished, unless in possession of a special permit."

Of the 50,000 Arab residents of Jaffa in this period, 15,000 remained, only to be subjected to widespread vandalism and violence. Within weeks of the Hagana's take-over of Jaffa on May 14, 1948, the population was reduced to 3,000.

From Jerusalem, US Consul William C. Burdett, who replaced Thomas Wasson, who was assassinated on May 23, 1948, cabled the Secretary of State on July 6, 1949, describing Palestinian refugees in terms of "despondency, misery, lack of hope and faith," with the "destruction of former standards of values," rendering them apt victims of communist propaganda.[5] Burdett continued, predicting that Israel "has no intention of allowing the return of any appreciable number of refugees except, perhaps, in return for additional territory....Arab houses and villages, including those in areas not given Israel by the partition decision, have been occupied to a large extent by new immigrants. Others have been deliberately destroyed. There is practically no room left. Arab quarters in Jerusalem, until recently a military zone, are now almost full and new immigrants are pouring in steadily."[6] And as Burdett concluded, "Israel eventually intends to obtain all of Palestine, but barring unexpected opportunities or internal crises will accomplish this objective gradually and without the use of force in the immediate future."

It was not only the Wassons, Lippincotts, Burdetts or Pinkertons who were in possession of such evidence. US officials in Washington had the same information. The US President, who had called for investigations of European Displaced Persons and insisted that 100,000 DPs be allowed to emigrate to Palestine, now faced Israel's denial of its own responsibility for the expulsion and flight of Palestinian refugees. The Israeli response became -- and remains -- the accepted formula in conventional accounts of the conflict.

"The Government of Israel must disclaim any responsibility for the creation of this problem. The charge that these Arabs were forcibly driven out by Israel authorities is wholly false; on the contrary, everything possible was done to prevent an exodus which was a direct result of the folly of the Arab states in organizing and launching a war of aggression against Israel. The impulse of the Arab civilian population to migrate from war areas, in order to avoid being involved in the hostilities, was deliberately fostered by Arab leaders for political motives. They did not wish the Arab population to continue to lead a peaceful existence in Jewish areas, and they wished to exploit the exodus as a propaganda weapon in surrounding Arab countries and in the outside world. This inhuman policy has now faced the governments concerned with practical problems for which they must assume full responsibility."[7]

The response of US officials who were deeply familiar with the course of Israeli policies was one of barely restrained bitterness as they contemplated the condition of Palestinian refugees and the future of what some described as a guerrilla war. Truman himself gave repeated signs of his frustration on the matter, as did State Department officials and US oil interests concerned with the overall impact of US policy. But there were other lines of policy evolving, those that viewed the new state's military capacity as a potentially important asset for US policy in the region.

It was in the same month in which the above declaration was made on the question of Palestinian refugees by Israel, that another kind of review was under way. This one came from the Acting U.S. Representative to the U.N., Philip Jessup, who wanted a clarification of US policy on Palestine prior to the UN's sending out its mediator, Bernadotte, to the region. As Jessup wrote, "although presumably the mediator will exercise a free hand, it is clear that the views of the United States will exercise a strong if not controlling influence on what is ultimately recommended or accepted."[8] What was also clear, as Jessup insisted in a later statement was that "our interests in the area will continue for an indefinite period..."[9]

Jessup then proceeded to outline his view of U.S. interests in Palestine which centered on his assessment of Israel's impressive military and political capacity, leading Jessup to support Israel's territorial expansion beyond the boundaries allotted in the 1947 Partition Plan, along with its demands for UN admission. And along the same vein, Jessup supported Israel's collaboration with Abdullah of Transjordan as a solution to the Palestine problem. As the US representative affirmed, "there will be a State of Israel;" and "there must also be an Arab State in Palestine,"[10] but Jessup failed to indicate who would control that state. Was it to be a Palestinian state controlled by Palestinians or one under the rule of Abdullah. What emerged from US sources was the latter.

Finally, there was the question of how Palestine/ Israel fit in US Middle East policy.

Jessup's explanation was straightforward:

"From the strategic viewpoint we assume that Palestine, together with the neighboring countries is a major factor presumably in any future major conflict this region would be of vital importance to US as a potential base area and with respect to our lines of communication. Presumably also the oil resources of the area are considered vital. It is our feeling that this last point may not perhaps have been dealt with adequately and frankly enough in official and public discussion of the Palestine question.

"From the economic viewpoint it is probable that with the exception of oil our trade and other economic relations with Palestine and the other Near East countries are not directly of any substantial importance. Indirectly, however, the economic stability and developing prosperity of Palestine and the Middle East under peaceful conditions could make a very substantial contribution to the economic recovery of the world generally and thus contribute to the economic welfare of the U.S. With respect to oil, we recognize that the oil supply from the area if of great importance in the European recovery program. Were it not for this factor, however, and the strategic importance of oil, we should probably not allow the economic importance of this commodity to condition our judgment substantially with regard to Palestine."[11]

Was Jessup alluding to those US officials who were persuaded of the urgency of 'conditioning' US policy on Palestine precisely because they believed that support of partition and statehood for Israel would place US oil interests at risk? Was he referring to those dealing with US oil policy who understood that such risks were effectively contained by the combination of the Saudi reluctance to break with US oil interests and the allied weakness of Arab regimes? Or was Jessup's concluding statement an unmistakable sign that he understood, as did the US military, that Israel was a promising asset in US strategic planning designed to guarantee US access and protection to Middle East oil?

It is useful to recall that by the spring of 1949 the US military, having reevaluated its prior position on Israel concluded that the nascent Israeli state with its, "small artificial harbor at Haifa, and an excellent although limited system of well-developed airfields and air bases," would be an asset to US Middle East policy.

CIA analysts were not as positive, warning of guerrilla war and an Israeli state permanently dependent on external support.

That was 1949. What of 2009? With all due recognition of the importance of not collapsing history or minimizing the significant changes that have transpired in the intervening years, remembering the earlier period is critical to an understanding of the foundations of the present conflict, including the role played by the US in the service of its interests.

Gaza in 2009 remains the mirror of 1948, a year in which it was utterly transformed as a result of the influx of Palestinian refugees. However altered by its political evolution and attendant frustrations and divisions,

Gaza's internal history is a chapter in the Palestinian struggle which is inseparable from the continuing Israeli-Palestinian conflict in which, as Jessup wrote earlier, the U.S. exercises "a strong if not controlling influence," and, as the Acting US Representative to the UN added, "our interests in the area will continue for an indefinite period...."

The crisis in Gaza is, thus far, contained within its perimeters, or at least its military dimension is so confined. But this cannot be said of its political impact which may prove to be no less savage. That the West Bank is directly affected, if not indirectly targeted, is evident, but the effect of the Gazan campaign extends to every Arab country that has been placed on notice, as a result. And it is not only the Arab states that are so affected.

The 'lessons' of Gaza will not be easily dispelled. What they reveal with a ferocity approved by the U.S. and carried out with due deliberation by its mightily militarized ally is that the campaign justified in the name of security is, in reality, a war waged without bounds against the 'wretched of the earth.'

[1] April 13, 1948, The Consul at Jerusalem (Wasson) to the Secretary of State, Foreign Relations of the United States (FRUS) 1948, Vol. V, part 2, p. 817.

[2] April 24, 1948, Lippincott, Haifa to Secretary of State, included in The Palestine Reference Files of Dean Rusk and Robert McClintock, 1947-1949, Record Group 59, National Archives and Records Service, General Services Administration, Washington 1981, Reel 10, no. 8955.

[3] June 23, 1948, The Consul at Haifa (Lippincott) to the Secretary of State, FRUS, 1948, V, part 2, p. 1138.

[4] Agreement between The Commander of the Hagana, Tel-Aviv District and the Palestinian members of the Jaffa Emergency Committee on May 13. 1948, included as an attachment to a Memorandum submitted by "The Jaffa and District Inhabitants Council," forwarded to the US Secretary State by Lowell C. Pinkerton, American Minister, American

Legation, Beirut, April 11, 1949, Cable No.65, in State Department Central Files on Lebanon, 1945-1949, RG 59 890E.00/4-1149.

[5] July 6, 1949, The Consul at Jerusalem (Burdett) to the Secretary of State, FRUS, 1949, VI, p. 1204.

[6] Ibid., p. 1205.

[7] July 27, 1948, The Acting United States Representative at the United Nations (Jessup) to the Secretary of State, FRUS, 1948, V, part 2, p. 1248.

[8] June 2, 1948, Memorandum by the Deputy United States Representative on the Security Council (Jessup) to the United States Representative at the United Nations (Austin), FRUS, 1948, V, part 2, p. 1088.

[9] July 1, 1948, The Acting United States Representative at the United Nations (Jessup) to the Secretary of State, FRUS, 1948, V, part 2, p. 1181.

[10] June 2, 1948, Memorandum by Jessup, op. cit., p. 1089.

[11] July 1, 1948, Jessup to Secretary of State, op. cit, p. 1181.

A "religious war" against Gentiles

ARE WE ANGRY YET? REFORM OR REVOLUTION IS EVIDENT

Israelis told to fight 'holy war' in Gaza, Many Israeli troops had the sense of fighting a "religious war" against Gentiles during the 22-day offensive in Gaza, according to a soldier who has highlighted the martial role of military rabbis during the operation. The soldier testified that the "clear" message of literature distributed to troops by the rabbinate was: "We are the Jewish people, we came to this land by a miracle, God brought us back to this land and now we need to fight to expel the Gentiles who are interfering with our conquest of this holy land." The claim comes in the detailed transcript of a post-war discussion by soldiers, publication of which has triggered a military police inquiry into allegations about the use of lethal firepower against unarmed civilians. The use of lethal firepower against unarmed civilians uh, that would be war crimes. Of course it was with the use of American weapons continually provided by the USA. Supported by the religious Evangelicans and zionist.-------- ARE WE ANGRY YET? REFORM OR REVOLUTION IS EVIDENT.---- PEACE AND JUSTICE:

Leverage U.S. military aid to halt Israeli settlements:

The settlement of Ariel, which sits deep inside the Palestinian Territory of the West Bank, voted overwhelmingly for Israeli Prime Minister Benjamin Netanyahu and his Likud Party in the recent elections. The reasons are straightforward: Likud has vowed to protect and expand settlements, and its platform denies the existence of a Palestinian state in the West Bank and Gaza.

These facts run contrary to stated U.S. policy toward the peace process, but the new government of Israel and the residents of Ariel and other settlements who voted for Likud do not seem to care.

Every American administration since Jimmy Carter's has taken a position against settlements in the West Bank. They are not only illegal under international law, but they also jeopardize Israel's long-term security, stability, and prospects for peace with its neighbors.

Settlements and the security structures that surround them debilitate the livelihoods of Palestinians, cut them off from each other, and make a viable Palestinian state unachievable. From 1994 to 2004, after the start of the Oslo peace process, which was based on the principle of two states, the settler population grew a striking 89 percent.

On a recent trip to the region, Secretary of State Hillary Rodham Clinton criticized settlement construction and the demolition of Palestinian homes in Jerusalem. Yet expansion plans continue to be developed by the Israeli Civil Administration.

Clearly, words have yet to alter the course of Israeli policies, and if the past is prologue, a Netanyahu-led government will not be helpful in ending construction. In fact, the last time Netanyahu was prime minister, settlement construction increased to its highest levels in 20 years.

When it comes to the Israeli-Palestinian conflict, we are running out of time to save a two-state solution. Waiting for "pro-peace" governments to be elected on both sides is like waiting for the planets to align. With the right wing on the rise in Israel and a fragmented Palestinian polity, the ideal configuration seems light-years away. Israel is on a crash course with an irreversible entanglement in Palestinian territory.

It's time for a new approach that will make it clear to the Israeli government that there must be a permanent freeze on settlement construction and expansion.

In 2007, the United States and Israel signed a memorandum of understanding guaranteeing Israel $30 billion in military assistance over the next decade. This assistance, however, has never been conditioned or leveraged to ensure compliance with U.S. policy on settlements.

By conditioning assistance on compliance with a complete and permanent freeze on settlement construction, the United States can send a clear message to Israel.

This message could also help Netanyahu. Since the domestic constituency that put him into power is sympathetic to settlement expansion, limitations on U.S. assistance can give Netanyahu the ability to argue that his hands are tied and that a settlement freeze is necessary.

If we are shipping our tax dollars overseas in these tough economic times, the least we should do is make sure they are being used to further U.S. objectives. If the United States truly is a friend to Israel, it should show some tough love, and conditioning aid is the right way to start.

WALK OUT, CAN NOT FACE THE TRUTH:

British delegates joined a dramatic diplomatic walkout today when President Ahmadinejad of Iran told a major UN conference against racism that the state of Israel had been founded "on the pretext of Jewish suffering" during the Second World War.

Around 20 delegates, including envoys from the UK, France, and Finland stood up and left the room at what was considered an anti-Semitic remark by the Iranian leader, who has repeatedly called for Israel to be wiped off the map.

Nine Western countries including Israel and the United States had already decided to boycott the conference entirely because its draft declaration endorsed the conclusions of an anti-racism conference in South Africa eight years ago in which Islamic nations pushed through a text equating Zionism with racism.

Even before the walkout, Mr Ahmadinejad's speech had been interrupted by three protesters dressed as clowns who where quickly bundled from the vast conference room at the Palais des Nations by guards.

Later, other protesters shouted down from the balcony as the Iranian president carried on his address.

Earlier today, Israel recalled its ambassador to Switzerland in protest at a brief meeting yesterday between Mr Ahmadinejad and his Swiss counterpart, Hans-Rudolf Merz.

The conference opened as Israel marks Holocaust Remembrance Day - which falls this year on the 120th anniversary of Adolf Hitler's birth. This morning the Israeli Prime Minister, Binyamin Netanyahu, told his Cabinet that while Israel commemorates the six million Jews slaughtered by the Nazis, "in Switzerland, the guest of honour is a racist and a Holocaust-denier who doesn't conceal his intention to wipe Israel off the face of this earth".

An Israeli Government official said that Ilan Elgar, the ambassador in Berne, had been "recalled for consultations" after the start of the Durban II conference and the meeting between Mr Ahmadinejad and Mr Merz, who holds Switzerland's rotating presidency.

"This is not a break in relations, but an expression of Israel's discontent for the lax Swiss attitude towards Iran," the official said.

The Obama administration announced at the weekend that it would boycott the meeting because its draft declaration makes reference to the text agreed in 2001 at the UN's first anti-racism conference in Durban, South Africa. That document was agreed after the United States and Israel walked out over attempts to liken Zionism - the movement to establish a Jewish state in the Holy Land - to racism.

Australia, Canada, Germany, Italy, the Netherlands, New Zealand and Poland joined the boycott.

Opening the conference this morning, the UN Secretary-General Ban Ki Moon urged the world to rally against the threat of intolerance.

"I fear that today's economic crisis, if not handled properly, could evolve into a full-scale political crisis marked by social unrest, weakened governments and angry publics who have lost faith in their leaders and their own future," Mr Ban said.

"In such circumstances, the consequences for communities already victimised by prejudice or exclusion could be frightening."

The UN chief said that he regretted the absence of the United States and the other boycotting member states.

"There comes a time to reaffirm our faith in fundamental human rights and the dignity and worth of us all," Mr Ban said.

The major sticking points in the draft final declaration prepared for the current meeting concern its implied criticism of Israel and an attempt by Muslim governments to remove all criticism of Islam, Sharia law, the Prophet Muhammad and other tenets of their faith.

The American decision to boycott the meeting has been given extra weight by the fact that it was taken by the country's first black president.

Speaking in Trinidad yesterday after attending the Summit of the Americas, Mr Obama said that he would love to be "involved in a useful conference that addressed continuing issues of racism and discrimination around the globe" but wanted to avoid a reprise of the Durban conference during which "folks expressed antagonism toward Israel in ways that were oftentimes completely hypocritical and counterproductive". However 98% of what has been stated is the "TRUTH", and the truth hurts some people.

Afghanistan is another false flag operation, the same
as Iraq. Israel, Mossad, and AIPAC influence the
American government again.

Israel can't attack Iran as they so desire to with out the USA military,
and Military Industrial complex
being directly involved.

Thus, we are moving more troops into Afghanistan,
for such involvement again. Does any of this represent
change in foreign policies that we were promised.

BRING ALL OUR TROOPS HOME.

Campaign reforms.
Election reforms.
Health care reform.
Energy reform.
Checks & Balance.
Accountability for officials.
Ear mark reform.
Rule of law.
Trade reform.
Lobby reform.
Foreign Policy reform.
Tax reform.
Spending reforms.
Regulation reform.

Everything needs an ACT of Congress to get anything
done for the Citizens of the United States.
Everything is in a "MESS" because we have not had
any real Act of Congress benefiting the American people. Only for
lobbies and foreign lobbies that have
been lining congress peoples pockets for years.

We need term limit reforms, and a quicker way of removing people from
office when there is no job performance.

Have we witnessed any real "ACTS OF CONGRESS?"
in the last twenty years that benefit the USA tax-payer. Haven't they
ALL been asleep at the switch?

It is time for the VOTERS to reform. Change will only
come about by changing the D. C. landscape

completely. VOTERS are the ones to do it.

2006 & 2008 Elections have been a good start,
how-ever corruption still remains. Remove them,
and charge & prosecute the crimes involved.

RESPONSIBILITIES OF OUR CITIZENS:

Unlike a dictatorship, a democratic government exists to serve the
people, but citizens in democracies must also agree to abide by the rules
and obligations by which they are governed. Democracies grant many
freedoms to their citizens including the freedom to dissent and criticize
the government.

Citizenship in a democracy requires participation, civility, and even
patience.

Democratic citizens recognize that they not only have rights, they have
responsibilities. They recognize that democracy requires an investment
of time and hard work – a government of the people demands constant
vigilance and support by the people.

Under some democratic governments, civic participation means that
citizens are required to serve on juries, or give mandatory military
or civilian national service for a period of time. Other obligations
apply to all democracies and are the sole responsibility of the citizen
– chief among these is respect for law. Paying one's fair share of taxes,
accepting the authority of the elected government, and respecting the
rights of those with differing points of view are also examples of citizen
responsibility. Democratic citizens know that they must bear the burden
of responsibility for their society if they are to benefit from its protection
of their rights.

There is a saying in free societies: you get the government you deserve. For
democracy to succeed, citizens must be active, not passive, because they
know that the success or failure of the government is their responsibility,
and no one else's. In turn, government officials understand that all citizens
should be treated equally and that bribery has no place in a democratic
government.

In a democratic system, people unhappy with their leaders are free to organize and peacefully make the case for change – or try to vote those leaders out of office at established times for elections.

Democracies need more than an occasional vote from their citizens to remain healthy. They need the steady attention, time, and commitment of large numbers of their citizens who, in turn, look to the government to protect their rights and freedoms.

Citizens in a democracy join political parties and campaign for the candidates of their choice.

They accept the fact that their party may not always be in power.

They are free to run for office or serve as appointed public officials for a time

They utilize a free press to speak out on local and national issues.

They join labor unions, community groups, and business associations.

They join private voluntary organizations that share their interests – whether devoted to religion, ethnic culture, academic study, sports, the arts, literature, neighborhood improvement, international student exchanges, or a hundred other different activities.

All these groups – no matter how close to or remote from government – contribute to the richness and health of their democracy.

Former Vice President used to claim that he constituted

a peculiar fourth branch of government unto himself, claiming executive privilege as part of the executive branch, while with the next breath refusing to obey executive branch record keeping laws?

Now we beginning to find out what that fourth branch of government actually was his own private worldwide assassination ring.

Somehow we don't recall the U.S. Constitution providing for such a fourth co-equal branch of our government.

Cheney was running his own personal assassination squad, reporting directly to himself.

Is there no level of treason outrageous enough to get one of the other two branches of government to confront these crimes against the Constitution? The justice department must immediately appoint a special prosecutor. Failing that, Congress must launch its own investigation, as called for by the always heroic Dennis Kucinich, to get to the bottom of this.

127 Journalist killed in Iraq, how many more assassinations, and who were they?

President Obama is ready to fight the lobbyists to pass his bold agenda. And the fight is officially on. Yesterday a top lobbyist called Obama's plan to transform our economy What we must understand is that we have only one
real enemy, our OWN defeatism, for that is all that stands between us and generating policy moving numbers.
 One need only observe how quickly Congress can move when there is real public outrage, like over the AIG bonus scandal, to realize that all we need to do is speak out in sufficient numbers to instantly have any policy change we want.
"devastating." If Obama's going to win this fight, he's going to need all of us fighting with him.
 It's a great time to be alive, and to be a progressive activist. We are living through a crisis, which at the same time presents us with the opportunity to pass great reforms to make life better for millions of people. Change is on the agenda, and together we are on the cutting edge of change, pushing the status quo towards true reforms.

The Big Four auditors knew what was going
Wall Street towers of fraud

Where were the giant accounting firms, the CPAs, and the rest of the accounting profession while the Wall Street towers of fraud, deception and cover-ups were fracturing our economy, looting and draining trillions of dollars of other peoples' money?
This is the licensed profession that is paid to exercise independent judgment with independent standards to give investors, pension funds,

mutual funds, and the rest of the financial world accurate descriptions of corporate financial realities.

It is now obvious that the accountants collapsed their own skill, integrity and self-respect faster and earlier than the collapse of Wall Street and the corporate barons. The accountants-both external and internal-could have blown the whistle on what Teddy Roosevelt called the "malefactors of great wealth."

The Big Four auditors knew what was going on with these complex, abstractly structured finance instruments, these collateralized debt obligations (CDOs) and other financial products too abstruse to label. They were on high alert after early warning scandals involving Long Term Capital Management, Enron, and others a decade or so ago.

These corporate casino capitalists used the latest tricks to cook the books with many of the on-balance sheet or off-balance sheet structured investment vehicles that metastasized big time in the first decade of this new century. These big firms can't excuse themselves for relying on conflicted rating companies, like Moody's or Standard & Poor, that gave triple-A ratings to CDO trenches in return for big fees. Imagine the conflict. After all, "prestigious" outside auditors were supposed to be on the inside incisively examining the books and their footnotes, on which the rating firms excessively relied.

Let's be specific with names. Carl Olson, chairman of the Fund for Stockowners Rights wrote in the letters column of The New York Times Magazine (January 28, 2009) that "PricewaterhouseCoopers O.K.'d AIG and FreddieMac. Deloitte & Touche certified Merrill Lynch and Bear Stearns. Ernst & Young vouched for Lehman Brothers and IndyMac Bank. KPMG assured over Countrywide and Wachovia. These 'Big Four' C.P.A. firms apparently felt they could act with impunity."

"Undoubtedly they knew that the state boards of accountancy," continued Mr. Olson, "which granted them their licenses to audit, would not consider these transgressions seriously. And they were right. Not one of them has taken up any serious investigation of the misbehaving auditors of the recent debacle companies."

"Misbehaving" is too kind a word. The "Big Four" destroyed their very reason for being by their involvement in these and other boondoggles that have made headlines and dragooned our federal government into bailing them out with disbursements, loans and guarantees totaling trillions of dollars. "Criminally negligent" is a better phrase for what these big accounting firms got rich doing-which is to look the other way.

Holding accounting firms like these accountable is very difficult. It got more difficult in 1995 when Congress passed a bill shielding them from investor lawsuits charging that they "aided and abetted" fraudulent or deceptive schemes by their corporate clients. Clinton vetoed the legislation, but Senator Chris Dodd (D-CT) led the fight to over-ride the veto.

Moreover, the under-funded and understaffed state boards of accountancy are dominated by accountants and are beyond inaction. What can you expect?

As for the Securities and Exchange Commission (SEC), "asleep at the switch for years" would be a charitable description of that now embarrassed agency whose mission is to supposedly protect savers and shareholders. This agency even missed the massive Madoff Ponzi scheme.

The question of accounting probity will not go away. In the past couple of weeks, the non-profit Financial Accounting Standards Board (FASB)-assigned to be the professional conscience of accountancy-buckled under overt pressure from Congress and the banks. It loosened the mark-to-market requirement to value assets at fair market value or what buyers are willing to pay.

This decision by the FASB is enforceable by the SEC and immediately "cheered Wall Street" and pushed big bank stocks upward. Robert Willens, an accounting analyst, estimated this change could boost earnings at some banks by up to twenty percent. Voilà, just like that. Magic!

Overpricing depressed assets may make bank bosses happy, but not investors or a former SEC Chairman, Arthur Levitt, who was "very disappointed" and called the FASB decision "a step toward the kind of opaqueness that created the economic problems that we're enduring today."

To show the deterioration in standards, banks tried to get the FASB and the SEC in the 1980s to water down fair-value accounting during the savings and loan failures. Then-SEC Chairman Richard Breeden refused outright. Not today.

Former SEC chief accountant, Lynn Turner, presently a reformer of his own profession, supports mark-to-market or fair value accounting as part of bringing all assets and liabilities, including credit derivatives, back on the balance sheets of the financial firms. He wants regulation of the credit rating agencies, mortgage originators and the perverse incentives that lead to making bad loans. He even wants the SEC to review these new financial products before they come to market, eliminating "hidden financing."

Now comes the life insurance industry, buying up some small banks to qualify for their own large federal bailouts for making bad, risky speculations.

The brilliant Joseph M. Belth, writing in his astute newsletter, the Insurance Forum (May 2009), noted that life insurers are lobbying state insurance departments to weaken statutory accounting rules so as to "increase assets and/or decrease liabilities." Some states have already caved. Again, voilà, suddenly there is an increase in capital. Magic. Here we go again.

Who among the brainy, head up accountants, in practice or in academia, will join with Lynn Turner and rescue this demeaned, chronically rubber-stamping "profession," especially the "Big Four," from its pathetic pretension for which tens of millions of people are paying dearly?

Nuclear restraints
April 9, 2009

It was nearly 25 years ago when Israeli nuclear scientist Mordechai Vanunu exposed his nation's secret nuclear weapons program to the world through The Sunday Times of London. Now, days before he is due to be released from captivity in Israel, an American president dared to envision a world free of nuclear weapons. In the Middle East, however, things seem to be heading in the opposite direction.

While the Israelis have stuck to a strategy of nuclear ambiguity, neither confirming or denying possession of nuclear weapons, experts around the globe estimate the Israeli stockpile to be in the range of 70 to 300 nuclear warheads, reports the Center for Strategic and International Studies. The Israelis have also taken pre-emptive and provocative steps to ensure nuclear dominance in the region by carrying out attacks in Iraq and Syria.

Despite the fact that the Israeli nuclear capability has contributed to the end of conventional interstate war in the region, animosity remains steady as battlefields shift. Increased asymmetrical warfare is on the rise and although Israel remains conventionally superior to its non-state enemies in the region, it has failed in eliminating the threats they pose.

Iran also continues to test Western patience by perpetuating its nuclear program. While Iran claims its nuclear program is peaceful, policymakers here often suspect otherwise.

The Middle East has enough problems and certainly does not need another, deadlier, weapons race. But an Iran-centric non-proliferation policy is myopic and dangerous and will likely lead the region into further destabilizing conflict.

A better approach is reviving an effort for a Middle East free of all weapons of mass destruction. Recalled in UN Security Council Resolution 687, the creation of a nuclear-free zone in the Middle East would go a great distance toward providing security for states in the region and re-establishing faith in the international legal system.

To do this, the international community, led by the United States, would have to put equal pressure on Iran and Israel to open their facilities for full inspection by the International Atomic Energy Agency and dismantle all nuclear weapons programs and eliminate all stockpiles.

This will not be easy for Israel to accept considering its history in the region and the solid track record of deterrence its weapons program has had with surrounding states.

However, these concerns can be allayed by strong security guarantees by the United States to retaliate against any state that launches a nuclear attack against Israel. A nuclear attack on Israel by a Muslim majority state is also deterred by the significant, and larger, number of Muslim kin who would be killed in such an attack.

This policy would have to go hand in hand with a resolution to the Israeli/Palestinian conflict, which has in recent years become a proxy battleground for the United States and Iran and has only resulted in the unnecessary deaths of countless innocents.

The alternatives to a nuclear-free zone in the Middle East are grim. It is unlikely that sanctions will halt a hurting but sustainable oil-exporting Iran, and military options cannot guarantee the desired outcome without the likelihood of ground operations or regional conflagration.

Eight years of disastrous U.S. foreign policy has contributed to the rise of a defensive Iran, the realignment of states in the Middle East, a perpetuated Israeli/Palestinian conflict and an increase in asymmetrical war throughout the region. The U.S. has a responsibility and a major national security and economic stake in setting the Middle East on a different course.

If President Barack Obama envisions a world free of nuclear weapons, he can begin by evenhandedly enforcing non-proliferation policy in the Middle East with Iran and Israel. Obama will get much further with this strategy than an Iran-only approach, which comes off to Middle Easterners as hypocritical, hegemonic and deceitful.

U.S. shipped 989 munitions containers to Israel week before Gaza invasion :

In the dying days of the Bush administration, and a week before Israel launched an aerial bombing campaign, followed by a land invasion of the Gaza Strip, the U.S. military shipped 989 containers of munitions to Israel.

Each container was 20-feet long with a total estimated net weight of 14,000 tonnes. The shipment reportedly reached Israel last month at Ashod, 40 kiometres north of Gaza. The huge arsenal of munitions will replenish those expended in the Gaza War.

According to Amnesty International in the UK, the shipment included white phosphorous.

The international organization says 300 of the containers had been unloaded at Ashod in March by a German cargo ship, Wehr Elb.

"We are sure that the consignment contained arms and munitions." We have a strong suspicion that it contained white phosphorous which has been used against civilians in Gaza," Brian Wood, head of Arms Control Campaign at Amnesty International in London said late this week.

"The cargo ship had been chartered and controlled by US Military Sealift Command. It left the USA for Israel on December 20, one week before the start of Israeli attacks on Gaza. The vessel was carrying 989 containers of munitions, each of them 20-feet long with a total estimated net weight of 14,000 tonnes," he said.

"The world community including the Palestinians should be able to know where the remaining 680 containers on board the Wehr Elbe have gone and why the US is not transparent about the final destination of the dangerous cargo.

"A Pentagon spokesperson confirmed to Amnesty International that "the unloading of the entire US munitions shipment was successfully completed at Ashdod on March 22," Wood pointed out.

The spokesperson had said the shipment was destined for a US pre-positioned munitions stockpile in Israel, he said. Under a US-Israel agreement, munitions from this stockpile may be transferred for Israeli use if necessary.

"There is a great risk that the new munitions may be used by the Israeli military to commit further violations of international law, like the ones committed during the war in Gaza," Wood said.

"Legally and morally, this US arms shipment should have been halted by the Obama administration given the extent of the evidence showing how military equipment and munitions of this kind were recently used by the Israeli forces for war crimes. Arms supplies in these circumstances are contrary to provisions in US law," he said.

An independent inquiry into possible abuses of international law by both sides in the Gaza conflict has been launched by the United Nations. The panel is being headed by Justice Richard J Goldstone of South Africa.

"The victims of this brutal conflict have a right to justice and reparation. The perpetrators on both sides must be held accountable if there is to be an end to the cycles of violence and impunity that have persisted for so long. There must be no excuse for either Israel or the Palestinians not to fully cooperate with the inquiry," Amnesty's Middle East and North Africa Program Director Malcolm Smart said this week.

During its December-January war on the occupied Gaza Strip, Israel killed 1,417 Palestinians, of whom 926 were civilians and 255 were non-combatant police officers, according to the Palestinian Centre for Human Rights. For additional details about Palestinian casualties read reports by Human rights organizations such as Amnesty International, Human Rights Watch, and the National Lawyers Guild have all published reports documenting Israel's misuse of U.S. weapons during its recent war on Gaza.

Yet, on top of the outrageous news that the United States delivered more weapons to Israel last month, President Obama is expected to request later this month $2.775 billion more in weapons for Israel in his detailed FY2010 budget request.

As Tax Day approaches, consider the fact that this amounts to $17.75 for each of the approximately 156 million individuals who filed a tax return with the IRS last year.

Is this how you want to see your tax dollars spent? If not, then take action. Demand the foreign policy CHANGE we were promised.

CON ARTIST, WHO ARE THEY??

They lie, cheat and fool people.
(Best example: The Republican Party)

Persons of any level of intelligence are vulnerable to deception by experienced con artists. Confidence tricks exploit human weaknesses like greed, dishonesty, vanity, but also virtues like honesty, compassion, or a naïve expectation of good faith on the part of the con artist. Just as there is no typical profile for swindlers, neither is there one for their victims. Virtually anyone can fall prey to fraudulent crimes. ... Certainly victims of high-yield investment frauds may possess a level of greed which exceeds their caution as well as a willingness to believe what they want to believe. However, not all fraud victims are greedy, risk-taking, self-deceptive individuals looking to make a quick dollar. Nor are all fraud victims naive, uneducated, or elderly. A confidence trick or confidence game (also known as a bunko, con, flim flam, gaffle, grift, hustle, scam, scheme, or swindle) is an attempt to defraud a person or group by gaining their confidence. Con artists make money through deception. They lie, cheat and fool people into thinking they've happened onto a great deal or some easy money, when they're the ones who'll be making money. If that doesn't work, they'll take advantage of our weaknesses -- loneliness, insecurity, poor health or simple ignorance. The only thing more important to a con artist than perfecting a con is perfecting a total lack of conscience. What does the average con artist look like? Despite what you may think, he isn't always a shady-looking character. A con artist is an expert at looking however he needs to look. If the con involves banking or investments, the con artist will wear a snappy suit. If it involves home improvement scams, he'll show up wearing well-worn work clothes. Even the basic assumption that the con is a "he" is incorrect: there are plenty of con women too. It would be impossible to catalogue every con, because con artists are inventive. While many cons are simply variations on ones that are hundreds of years old, new technologies and laws give con artists the opportunity to create original scams. Many cons tend to fall into a few general categories, however: street cons, business cons, Internet cons, health cons and self improvement cons. Tired of working for your money? Cheat the system and cheat other people by becoming a con artist! Scam and swindle your way to the top. Become a preacher, politician, or a used car salesman, you will be well on your way.

The Heritage Foundation's survey:
Co-sponsors of Fascism.

RE: The recent survey conducted by:
The Heritage Foundation
Attn: Membership Office
214 Massachusetts Avenue, NE
Washington, DC 20002

SPOTLIGHT from Townhall.com

Co-sponsors of Fascism.

Their attacks on our president are out of order.

The Republican Party and conservative right lost the election and will continue to lose.

The eight years you had total control, and did nothing but leave the Country in a complete MESS.

If you want to do something for the Country.
Sit on your fat asses, and keep your mouths shut.

We hope that all members of the past administration end up in Jail (Prison) where they belong.

75% of the corruption in Washington DC involves the republican, AIPAC, corporate crime syndicate.---

Call this a survey? Who are you kidding?

No Republican should be re-elected. All are WAR PROFITEERS.---

See the bias survey below.

100 Days: The Heritage Foundation's Survey on the Obama Agenda
Your answers to this important survey will help America's leading conservative policy organization further develop our response to the liberal agenda promoted by the administration and Congress. And it will allow us to refine dictatorship for America, our ten-year campaign to get the nation back on track through a return to crummy, conservative principles.

Survey Questions
1. How do you think President Barack Obama is governing?

as a moderate, trying to unite Americans--
as a radical, moving America to the left--
moderate in some areas, radical in others--

2. Are you worried that the left will make good on its threats against conservative speech?

Yes --
No --
Undecided--

3. Do you believe the left presents a threat to our national security?

Yes--
No--
Undecided --

4. Do you think leftists in and outside of Congress will succeed in prosecuting Bush administration officials for "war crimes"?

Yes --
No--
Undecided --

5. Do you think leftist policies are putting our free-market economic system in danger?

Yes --
No--
Undecided--

6. What do you think are the most important issues for conservatives to focus on in the coming year? (You may check more than one.)

blocking leftist attempts to weaken our national security --

promoting free-market solutions to our economic problems --

preventing liberals from raising taxes--

preventing a government takeover of our health care--

blocking confirmation of radical judges--

stopping amnesty for illegal aliens--

preserving free speech for conservatives --

promoting a strong effort in the war on Islamist terrorism --

protecting traditional marriage --

blocking measures that give labor unions massive power--

producing more oil, gas, and nuclear power --

7. From which media do you get most of your news? (You may check more than one.)

The TV networks --

Cable news stations --

Newspapers --

Magazines --

Radio news --

Radio Talk Shows --

The Internet-- .

Republican senators filibuster EVERYTHING:

There was a story this week that Republican senators were threatening to "go nuclear" and filibuster EVERYTHING (as if they were not already doing that) if the Justice department released the secret memos that the Bush administration had drafted to their own evil specifications to say that torture was OK. If these apparently flimsy, self-serving documents were supposed to stand as a get out of jail free card for the Bush/Cheney torturers, they must be pretty damning stuff.

Indeed, if this was supposed to be their defense for war crimes, war crimes that have made us all dramatically less safe by exponentially ramping up hatred for the U.S. all over the world, they should be proud to display their defense in the full light of day. But it is Republican members of Congress who are desperately trying to get Obama to keep their filthy, treasonous secrets with them, so we must speak out to them in particular. Shame on the so-called rule of law crowd ... for abject, irredeemable shame. And on us as well if unless we demand the immediate release of these legal hack jobs.

Hold their feet to/in the fire!!

Show your support for the best president we have seen in any of our life times.

PRESIDENT BARACK OBAMA.

Here are the latest updates for rwaldron@stny.rr.com

"MuzzleWatch" - 1 new article

The "Jewish Conspiracy" behind the Durban Review Conference
More Recent Articles
Search MuzzleWatch
The "Jewish Conspiracy" behind the Durban Review Conference
Michael Jordan of the Jewish Telegraphic Agency has an interesting piece today about the hesitance of the UN High Commissioner's Office to actually name the groups behind the campaign to marginalize the Durban Review Conference. Jordan writes:

It's no secret who was behind the effort to discredit the 2009 Durban Review Conference in Geneva.

For nearly a year before the anti-racism confab, Jewish and pro-Israel groups lobbied hard to get Western countries to boycott the gathering, which they said was certain to treat Israel unfairly, just as the first Durban conference had done in 2001.

But why, when pressed, do UN officials give such vague answers?

This time, however, the Jews actually did conspire, albeit openly, to sabotage the conference.

…But for the most part, Durban II's organizers and participants did not want to point the finger at the Jews for the anti-Durban effort for fear of being labeled anti-Semites.

"I can't tell you exactly who the lobby is," Pillay said in a March 12 interview with Australia's ABC.net. "I can just pick out that it seems to be one source putting out this wrong information and labeling this review conference as 'hate fest.'"

In an earlier piece, Jordan reports a story that illustrates exactly the impossible dynamic faced by the UN office, and how, like a powerless female character in a film who threatens to yell 'rape' if someone gets too close, some Jewish groups are only too happy to cry 'anti-Semite' if you get too close. In some ways, its the nuclear option for powerless people. (Worse, as I have amply documented, these Jewish/Israel lobby groups sponsored a range of sessions demonizing and attacking the UN, Arabs, Muslims, Iran and Palestinians, all with Orwellian titles about fighting bigotry and anti-Semitism.)

The head of an official NGO alliance at the UN told me groups have an agreement not to protest inside of the United Nations, and that if they do, it is standard practice to revoke the group's accreditation. When the UN tried to do just that to the European Union of Jewish Students, which disrupted the conference at various moments, the chair boasted that one threat to send out a press statement made all the difference:

Another student group, the European Union of Jewish Students, had learned April 21 that its accreditation was pulled after some members had yelled insults at Ahmadinejad from the gallery.

But the EUJS, which also has formal, permanent accreditation to the United Nations, protested that the entire group shouldn't be punished for the actions of a few. EUJS Chairman Jonas Karpantschof said he told U.N. officials he would issue a news release if the accreditation weren't reinstated, and it soon was.

"It would have looked really bad," he said, "for the U.N. to take away badges from Jewish students on Yom Hashoah at an anti-racism conference."

Jordan himself feeds the dynamic in the same article, called "Malcolm X's daughter: 'Zionist agitators' bothered at Durban II. The article comes complete with an angry looking photo of Malaak Shabazz, who complained about ""Zionist agitators" at one event who were " juvenile, nasty and aggressive." In fact, friends from Canada's Independent Jewish Voices were in the room when the students were acting in threatening ways and stuck a camera right in Shabazz's face. One can only assume that as Malcolm X's daughter, an "angry black Muslim woman", she was right out of central casting for a depiction of the scary, anti-Semitic, mean Durban Review delegates.

I went to an Israel rally where the audience was exhorted to yell, "I am a Zionist" half a dozen times. But Shabazz, who was literally right when she called these young students "Zionist agitators", is now part of the massive anti-Jewish hate-fest because she used the phrase.

IMPORTANT TO NOTE:

Remember when you go to the voting booth:

The Bankers that helped cause the mess--Are Republican.

The Wall Street Brokers that ripped you off--Are Republican.

The Oil companies profitting on you--Are Republican.

The drug companies with excessive Profits--Are Republican.

The companies that out-sourced your jobs--Are Republican.

The Insurance Companies, that lobby against
Health Care reform are of course--Republican.

The War profiteers, and no bid contractors--Are Republican.

Not all, but 75% of the corrupt with-in our government--are Republican.

WHY! would any moral, intelligent, ethical, citizen of the USA ever vote for a Republican again.
Their agenda is not for the good of us average Americans.

The Haircut

One day a florist goes to a barber for a haircut. After the cut he asks about his bill and the barber replies,' I cannot accept money from you... I'm doing community service this week.' The florist was pleased and left the shop.
When the barber goes to open his shop the next morning there is a 'thank you' card and a dozen roses waiting for him at his door.
Later, a cop comes in for a haircut, and when he tries to pay his bill, the barber
again replies, 'I cannot accept money from you. I'm doing community service this week.' The cop is happy and leaves the shop.
The next morning when the barber goes to open up there is a 'thank you' card and a dozen donuts waiting for him at his door.
Later that day, a college professor comes in for a haircut, and when he tries to pay his bill, the barber again replies, 'I cannot accept money from you. I'm doing community service this week.' The professor is very happy and leaves the shop.
The next morning when the barber opens his shop, there is a 'thank you' card and a dozen different books, such as 'How to Improve Your Business' and Becoming More Successful'.
Then, a Congressman comes in for a haircut, and when he goes to pay his bill the barber again replies, 'I cannot accept money from you. I'm doing community service this week.' The Congressman is very happy and leaves the shop.
The next morning when the barber goes to open up, there are a dozen Congressmen lined up waiting for a free haircut?

And that, my friends, illustrates the fundamental difference between the citizens of our country and the members of our Congress.

Dedication to:

MY FRIEND, MY BROTHER:

Dearest Mel:

My friend, my brother, how I wish you were here to see the advancements of diversity in America today.

Melvin Parr was an African American that we invited into our home back in 1960. He needed a home, friends, and family so he could finish High School, and to continue participating in high school sports. Melvin graduated from Randolph, NY High School in 1961,after which his interest was civil rights, to be an equal with-in our society. He participated in marches with Dr. Martin Luther King in Washington DC.

Eventually Mel moved to Chicago,IL, married and raised a family. He became ill with lupus, kidney failure, and passed with heart failure 2001.

Melvin and I communicated often. We both wished for better understanding of racial issues.I knows he would be very active in the Obama campaign if he were here today. Not based on race itself, but because of equal abilities, knowledge, and capabilities to lead. Most importantly above the normal qualifications, with an agenda for all Americans not just the RICH.

Thus I have done all I possibly can do for all America, by campaigning for Obama / Biden. A campaign not accepting funds from special interest. A team that will end a needless WAR, and needless killing of civilians.

Also a team that will work at ending the Israeli-Palestine conflict. A team that will negotiate fairly in Foreign Affairs. That will change the policies of the Rich getting richer, and the poor getting poorer.

That equal rights include women, blacks, Hispanics, Asians, Native Americans, the elderly and youth, us all.

Including equal pay, for equal work.

I'm retired from Law enforcement, and corrections.

I have seen a lot of advancement since 1960. BUT there is more work to be done that benefits us all.

Your friend, and Brother;

Ron
(A Caucasian as if it matters)

ABOUT THE AUTHOR

I retired after serving several years in the criminal Justice fields of law enforcement, Public defenders office, Security, and prison correctional.

An interest developed for criminal justice after the assassination of President John F. Kennedy.
After serving in the US Army, I joined the police department, I'm high mileage, and been to a few fairs during my career, took me to several areas around the Country. Regardless of the outcome of investigations and hearings, there is enough evidence that the American people, needed to force change.

ALL AMERICAN PEOPLE: African, Hispanic, Asian, Native, Poor and middle class Americans needed to unite and demanded CHANGE. We voiced it to no avail 2006 elections, we then demanded it 2008 elections. Please help our president for such change "Barack Obama".

GIVE HIM ALL THE SUPPORT YOU POSSIBLY CAN.

YES, this is all about America, not the author.

PEACE 4 ALL

www.ingramcontent.com/pod-product-compliance
Lightning Source LLC
Chambersburg PA
CBHW02024129O526
45784CB00003B/1062